Insights You Need from

Business is changing. Will you adapt or be left behind?

Get up to speed and deepen your understanding of the topics that are shaping your company's future with the **Insights You Need from Harvard Business Review** series. Featuring HBR's smartest thinking on fast-moving issues—blockchain, cybersecurity, AI, and more—each book provides the foundational introduction and practical case studies your organization needs to compete today and collects the best research, interviews, and analysis to get it ready for tomorrow.

You can't afford to ignore how these issues will transform the landscape of business and society. The Insights You Need series will help you grasp these critical ideas—and prepare you and your company for the future.

Books in the series include:

Agile

Artificial Intelligence

Blockchain

Climate Change

Customer Data and Privacy

Cybersecurity

Monopolies and Tech Giants

Strategic Analytics

The Year in Tech, 2021

Insights You Need from
Harvard Business Review

MONOPOLIES + TECH GIANTS

Insights You Need from
Harvard Business Review

MONOPOLIES + TECH GIANTS

Harvard Business Review Press
Boston, Massachusetts

Copyright 2020 Harvard Business School Publishing Corporation
All rights reserved
Printed in the United States of America

10 9 8 7 6 5 4 3 2 1

The web addresses referenced in this book were live and correct at the time of the book's publication but may be subject to change.

Library of Congress Cataloging-in-Publication Data

Title: Monopolies and tech giants.
Other titles: Insights you need from Harvard Business Review.
Description: Boston, Massachusetts : Harvard Business Review Press, [2020] | Series: Insights you need from Harvard Business Review | Includes index.
Identifiers: LCCN 2019046753 (print) | LCCN 2019046754 (ebook) | ISBN 9781633699014 (paperback) | ISBN 9781633699021 (ebook)
Subjects: LCSH: Monopolies. | Big business. | Technology—Economic aspects. | Competition. | Internet industry. | High technology industries.
Classification: LCC HD2757.2 .M635 2020 (print) | LCC HD2757.2 (ebook) | DDC 338.8/2—dc23
LC record available at https://lccn.loc.gov/2019046753
LC ebook record available at https://lccn.loc.gov/2019046754

ISBN: 978-1-63369-901-4
eISBN: 978-1-63369-902-1

Contents

Contents

Section 2

The Future of Antitrust and Regulation

Section 3
Competing Against Giants

Contents

Introduction

HOW CAN YOU COMPETE AGAINST WORLD-DOMINATING GIANTS?

This book isn't another celebration of Apple's genius or Amazon's disciplined multidecade vision. Nor is it a breathless screed against Google's anticompetitive practices or Facebook's repeated policy disasters. You've probably read those books already, and they haven't given you the answers you and your business need.

The tech giants—love them, hate them, or just fear them—are here to stay and continuing to grow in power and influence. They're using their sprawling networks and vast advantages in data collection and AI to expand into industries ranging from groceries to personal finance to education. They're acquiring their competitors left and right, and pushing many more into bankruptcy. If you want your business to *exist* in a few years, let alone to be thriving and growing, you need to be thinking now about how your company will fit in once the new tech monopolies have finished rewriting all the rules.

You know them by many names: the frightful five, FAANGs, BATs, the big nine, the tech titans. There's no comprehensive list, but it's safe to say that Alibaba, Alphabet, Amazon, Apple, Baidu, Facebook, and Tencent are high among them. Microsoft seemed to be out of the club for a while, but it's back (perhaps it was never really gone). Uber and Lyft were ascending into the pantheon until the grease-and-gridlock challenges of the transportation industry, a disappointing IPO, and good old-fashioned mismanagement lopped a few inches off their unicorn horns.

Their leaders have been equally lionized and demonized in the business press and even on film. Steve Jobs is seen as both the patron saint of ecosystems and an autocratic leader no *Harvard Business Review* reader from this decade would want to emulate. Mark Zuckerberg's reputation has evolved from an idealistic, brilliant wunderkind into a petulant billionaire ostrich, willing to turn a blind eye to the real-world problems to retain Facebook's share of advertising dollars. Their philanthropic ventures and side projects have at times been tinged with sci-fi fantasies (for example, Jeff Bezos's plans for billions—or is it trillions?—of moon colonists). Yet some, like the Gates Foundation's global health efforts, may one day be worthy of the Nobel Peace Prize.

As their customers, both at work and at home, we can see the contradictions. We love their products. We hate what they do to our attention spans and to small businesses. We try, desperately, to make our companies more like them, even as the tech-bro culture and antiworker policies make us queasy. We break up with them. We come crawling back. We renounce and denounce them on their own platforms, delete our accounts, and are left with the nagging feeling that we can never really quit them. Even a small task like this—typing a dash—uses Apple hardware using Microsoft software on an Amazon Web Services cloud. Are you ever *not* using them? Are they ever *not* collecting your data and processing it with their AI engines? Their products are like oxygen. We can hold our breaths, but only briefly. Can your company compete against *air*?

Against this backdrop, a "techlash" is taking place. The behemoths' own rank-and-file employees are protesting in the streets, and some of their own founders are penning scathing statements to express their regret about what they helped create. Politicians across the spectrum worldwide are trying to land a solid punch on the mega-firms. Could new regulations or antitrust policies hinder their growth? So far, with each censure, the giants have paid up, tweaked their policies, and pushed ahead. Never before has a multibillion-dollar fine seemed so much like a slap on the wrist. Some of these firms have made concrete steps toward self-regulation, and a number demonstrate an understanding that they must lead responsibly for the good of their own ecosystems and for society. But don't count on the slim hope that the public sector will swoop in to referee or break up big tech.

Monopolies and Tech Giants: The Insights You Need from Harvard Business Review will help you navigate this new business landscape. Section 1 explores the business and ethical implications of a few hub firms capturing a disproportionate share of value and shaping our economic futures. It presents a case study from the near future of what the automotive industry might look like when smart, connected cars are run by the tech giants' software. Finally, it discusses the degree to which competition is being dampened due to consolidation across industries.

Last century's regulatory policies are not up to the task of reining in the excesses of today's digital superpowers. Section 2 looks ahead to the future of antitrust. It covers the potential catastrophic consequences of a monopoly on personal data. You'll read arguments for strengthening the traditional tools of antitrust enforcement, explorations of unconventional new techniques, and ideas about why government intervention might not achieve its intended effects.

Section 3 gets to the heart of the matter: What should your business do, right now, to ensure its survival alongside the giants? They have changed the rules of strategy, and the choices you face aren't simple. For some companies, the answer is to become bigger, broader, faster, more like the tech monopolies. Others will deliberately remain small and focused, honing a few unmatchable capabilities, brands, or services. Many will have to choose whether they'll participate in the superpowers' ecosystems or create (or buy) their own. And no matter the strength of your company now, it will have to find new ways to innovate and reinvent itself to keep pace with the ever-evolving mega-firms.

Consider these questions as you prepare your company for the challenge:

- What role do the tech giants play in your industry now? Have they already reshaped it?

- Is the giants' role in your industry primarily as a network creator or platform provider? Or do they provide products or services that compete directly with your offerings?

- What capabilities and advantages do your company and other incumbents in your industry have that are preventing the superpowers from entering (or taking over) your industry? How durable are these advantages?

- What role could domestic or international antitrust or data-privacy regulation play in your industry? Will it affect the largest and smallest companies in different ways?

If you and your organization haven't confronted these questions yet, let this book spark the conversations necessary to move you forward. Thriving in a business environment dominated by a handful of huge tech companies will require endless perseverance, grit, and imagination. The future version of *your* company, the one that is holding its own against the tech giants and growing—or perhaps even challenging them on their own turf—may not look like what you see around you today. Start creating that future now.

Section 1

THE DOMINANCE OF MEGA-FIRMS

1

MANAGING OUR HUB ECONOMY

by Marco Iansiti and Karim R. Lakhani

The global economy is coalescing around a few digital superpowers. We see unmistakable evidence that a winner-take-all world is emerging in which a small number of "hub firms"—including Alibaba, Alphabet/Google, Amazon, Apple, Baidu, Facebook, Microsoft, and Tencent—occupy central positions. While creating real value for users, these companies are also capturing a disproportionate and expanding share of the value, and that's shaping our collective economic future. The very same technologies that promised to democratize business are now threatening to make it more monopolistic.

Beyond dominating individual markets, hub firms create and control essential connections in the networks that pervade our economy. Google's Android and related technologies form "competitive bottlenecks"; that is, they own access to billions of mobile consumers that other product and service providers want to reach. Google can not only exact a toll on transactions but also influence the flow of information and the data collected. Amazon's and Alibaba's marketplaces also connect vast numbers of users with large numbers of retailers and manufacturers. Tencent's WeChat messaging platform aggregates a billion global users and provides a critical source of consumer access for businesses offering online banking, entertainment, transportation, and other services. The more users who join these networks, the more attractive (and even necessary) it becomes for enterprises to offer their products and services through them. By driving increasing returns to scale and controlling crucial competitive bottlenecks, these digital superpowers can become even mightier, extract disproportionate value, and tip the global competitive balance.

Hub firms don't compete in a traditional fashion—vying with existing products or services, perhaps with improved features or lower cost. Rather, they take the network-based assets that have already reached scale in one setting and then use them to enter another industry and "re-architect" its competitive structure—transforming it from product-driven to network-driven. They plug adjacent industries into the same competitive bottlenecks they already control.

For example, the Alibaba spin-off Ant Financial does not simply offer better payment services, a better credit card, or an improved investment management service; it builds on data from Alibaba's already vast user base to commoditize traditional financial services and reorganize a good chunk of the Chinese financial sector around the Ant Financial platform. The three-year-old service already has over half a billion users and plans to expand well beyond China. Similarly, Google's automotive strategy does not simply entail creating an improved car; it leverages technologies and data advantages (many already at scale from billions of mobile consumers and millions of advertisers) to change the structure of the auto industry itself. (Disclosure: Both of us work or have worked with some of the firms mentioned in this article.)

If current trends continue, the hub economy will spread across more industries, further concentrating data, value, and power in the hands of a small number of firms employing a tiny fraction of the workforce. Disparity in firm valuation and individual wealth already causes widespread resentment. Over time, we can expect consumers, regulators, and even social movements to take an increasingly hostile stand against this concentration of value and economic connectivity. In a painfully ironic turn, after creating unprecedented opportunity across the global economy, digitization—and the trends it has given rise to—could exacerbate already dangerous levels of income inequality, undermine the economy, and even lead to social instability.

Can these trends be reversed? We believe not. The "hub economy," as we will argue, is here to stay. But most companies will not become hubs, and they will need to respond astutely to the growing concentration of hub power. Digitizing operating capabilities will not be enough. Digital messaging platforms, for example, have already dealt a blow to telecom service providers; investment advisers still face threats from online financial-services companies. To remain competitive, companies will need to use their assets and capabilities differently, transform their core businesses, develop new revenue opportunities, and identify areas that can be defended from encroaching hub firms and others rushing in from previously disconnected economic sectors. Some companies have started on this path—Comcast, with its Xfinity platform, is a notable example—but the majority, especially those in traditional sectors, still need to master the implications of network competition.

Most importantly, the very same hub firms that are transforming our economy must be part of the solution—and their leaders must step up. As Mark Zuckerberg articulated in his Harvard commencement address in 2017, "we have a level of wealth inequality that hurts everyone." Business as usual is not a good option. Witness the public concern about the roles that Facebook and Twitter played in the 2016 U.S. presidential election, Google's challenges with global regulatory bodies, criticism of Uber's culture and operating policies, and complaints that Airbnb's rental practices are racially discriminatory and harmful to municipal housing stocks, rents, and pricing.

Thoughtful hub strategies will create effective ways to share economic value, manage collective risks, and sustain the networks and communities we all ultimately depend on. If carmakers, major retailers, or media companies continue to go out of business, massive economic and social dislocation will ensue. And with governments and public opinion increasingly attuned to this problem, hub strategies that foster a more stable economy and united society will drive differentiation among the hub firms themselves.

We are encouraged by Facebook's response to the public outcry over "fake news"—hiring thousands of dedicated employees, shutting down tens of thousands of phony accounts, working with news sources to identify untrue claims, and offering guides for spotting false information. Similarly, Google's YouTube division invests in engineering, artificial intelligence, and human resources and collaborates with NGOs to ensure that videos promoting political extremists and terrorists are taken down promptly.

A real opportunity exists for hub firms to truly lead our economy. This will require hubs to fully consider the long-term societal impact of their decisions and to prioritize their ethical responsibilities to the large economic ecosystems that increasingly revolve around them. At the same time, the rest of us—whether in established enterprises or startups, in institutions or communities—will need to serve as checks and balances, helping to shape the hub economy by providing critical, informed input and, as needed, pushback.

The Digital Domino Effect

The emergence of economic hubs is rooted in three principles of digitization and network theory. The first is Moore's law, which states that computer processing power will double approximately every two years. The implication is that performance improvements will continue driving the augmentation and replacement of human activity with digital tools. This affects any industry that has integrated computers into its operations—which pretty much covers the entire economy. And advances in machine learning and cloud computing have only reinforced this trend.

The second principle involves connectivity. Most computing devices today have built-in network connectivity that allows them to communicate with one another. Modern digital technology enables the sharing of information at near-zero marginal cost, and digital networks are spreading rapidly. Metcalfe's law states that a network's value increases with the number of nodes (connection points) or users—the dynamic we think of as network effects. This means that digital technology is enabling significant growth in value across our economy, particularly as open-network connections allow for the recombination of business offerings, such as the migration from payment tools to the broader financial services and insurance that we've seen at Ant Financial.

But while value is being created for everyone, value capture is getting more skewed and concentrated. This is because in networks, traffic begets more traffic, and as certain nodes become more heavily used, they attract additional attachments, which further increases their importance. This brings us to the third principle, a lesser-known dynamic originally posited by the physicist Albert-László Barabási: the notion that digital-network formation naturally leads to the emergence of positive feedback loops that create increasingly important, highly connected hubs. As digital networks carry more and more economic transactions, the economic power of network hubs, which connect consumers, firms, and even industries to one another, expands. Once a hub is highly connected (and enjoying increasing returns to scale) in one sector of the economy (such as mobile telecommunications), it will enjoy a crucial advantage as it begins to connect in a new sector (automobiles, for example). This can, in turn, drive more and more markets to tip, and the many players competing in traditionally separate industries get winnowed down to just a few hub firms that capture a growing share of the overall economic value created—a kind of digital domino effect.

This phenomenon isn't new. But in recent years, the high degree of digital connectivity has dramatically sped up the transformation. Just a few years ago, cell phone manufacturers competed head-to-head for industry leadership in a traditional product market without appreciable network effects. Competition led to innovation and differentiation, with a business model delivering healthy profitability at scale for a dozen or so major competitors. But with the introduction of iOS and Android, the industry began to tip away from its hardware centricity to network structures centered on these multisided platforms. The platforms connected smartphones to a large number of apps and services. Each new app makes the platform it sits on more valuable, creating a powerful network effect that in turn creates a more daunting barrier to entry for new players. Today Motorola, Nokia, BlackBerry, and Palm are out of the mobile phone business, and Google and Apple are extracting the lion's share of the sector's value. The value captured by the large majority of complementors—the app developers and third-party manufacturers—is generally modest at best.

The domino effect is now spreading to other sectors and picking up speed. Music has already tipped to Apple, Google, and Spotify. E-commerce is following a similar path: Alibaba and Amazon are gaining more share and moving into traditional brick-and-mortar strongholds like groceries (witness Amazon's acquisition of Whole Foods). We've already noted the growing power of WeChat in messaging and communications; along with Facebook and others, it's challenging traditional telecom service providers. On-premise computer and software offerings are losing ground to the cloud services provided by Amazon, Microsoft, Google, and Alibaba. In financial services, the big players are Ant, Paytm, Ingenico, and the independent startup Wealthfront; in home entertainment, Amazon, Apple, Google, and Netflix dominate.

Where are powerful hub firms likely to emerge next? Health care, industrial products, and agriculture are three contenders. But let's examine how the digital domino effect could play out in another prime candidate, the automotive sector, which in the United States alone provides more than seven million jobs and generates close to a trillion dollars in yearly sales.

Re-Architecting the Automotive Sector

As with many other products and services, cars are now connected to digital networks, essentially becoming rolling information and transaction nodes. This connectivity is reshaping the structure of the automotive industry. When cars were merely products, car sales were the main prize. But a new source of value is emerging: the connection to consumers in transit. Americans spend almost an hour, on average, getting to and from work every day, and commutes keep getting longer. Auto manufacturers, responding to consumer demand, have already given hub firms access to dashboard screens in many cars; drivers can use Apple or Google apps on the car's built-in display instead of on their smartphones. If consumers embrace self-driving vehicles, that one hour of consumer access could be worth hundreds of billions of dollars in the United States alone.

Which companies will capitalize on the vast commercial potential of a new hour of free time for the world's car commuters? Hub firms like Alphabet and Apple are first in line. They already have bottleneck assets like maps and advertising networks at scale, and both are ready to create super-relevant ads pinpointed to the car's passengers and location. One logical add-on feature for autonomous vehicles would be a "Drive there" button that appears when an ad pops up (as already happens on Google's Waze app); pressing it would order the car to head to the touted destination.

In a future when people are no longer behind the wheel, cars will become less about the driving experience and more about the apps and services offered by automobiles as they ferry passengers around. Apart from a minority of cars actually driven for fun, differentiation will lessen, and the vehicle itself might well become commoditized. That will threaten manufacturers' core business: The car features that buyers will care most about—software and networks—will be largely outside the automakers' control, and their price premiums will go down.

The transformation will also upend a range of connected sectors—including insurance, automotive repairs

FIGURE 1-1

The connected-car ecosystem

Three software platforms—Android Auto, Apple CarPlay, and, to a lesser extent, OpenCar—dominate the market for integrating smartphone functionality into vehicles. They constitute powerful bottleneck assets because they have scores of supply-chain partners (left) and they enable other stakeholders (right) to reach consumers. (Note: The companies, apps, and regulators listed are selected examples only.)

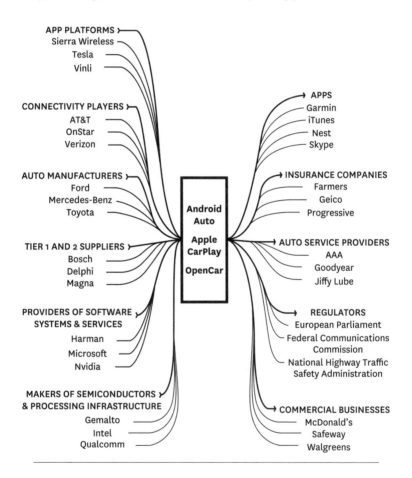

and maintenance, road construction, law enforcement, and infrastructure—as the digital dominos continue to fall. (See figure 1-1.)

For existing auto manufacturers, the picture is grim but not hopeless. Some companies are exploring a pay-per-use model for their cars and are acquiring, launching, or partnering with car-as-a-service providers. GM, for one, invested $500 million in the ride-sharing service Lyft, and its luxury-car division is now offering a monthly car subscription service. Daimler launched a car-sharing business called car2go. Several manufacturers have also invested in their own research into driverless vehicles or partnered with external providers.

Beyond these business-model experiments, automakers will need to play as the hubs do, by participating in the platform competition that will determine value capture in the sector. At least for the moment, alternatives to Google and Apple are scarce. One example is OpenCar, which was acquired by Inrix, a traditional auto supplier. Unlike Apple CarPlay and Google's Android Auto, which limit automaker-specific customization and require access to proprietary car data, the OpenCar framework is fully controlled by the car manufacturer. To take on the established giants, we believe that OpenCar and Inrix will have to develop an effective advertising or commerce platform or adopt some other indirect monetization strategy—and to do that, they'll probably need to partner with companies that have those capabilities.

To reach the scale required to be competitive, automotive companies that were once fierce rivals may need to join together. Here Technologies, which provides precision mapping data and location services, is an interesting example. Here has its roots in Navteq, one of the early online mapping companies, which was first bought by Nokia and later acquired by a consortium of Volkswagen, BMW, and Daimler (the multibillion-dollar price tag may have been too high for any single carmaker to stomach). Here provides third-party developers with sophisticated tools and APIs for creating location-based ads and other services. The company represents an attempt by auto manufacturers to assemble a "federated" platform and, in doing so, neutralize the threat of a potential competitive bottleneck controlled by Google and Apple. The consortium could play a significant role in preventing automotive value capture from tipping completely toward existing hub firms.

Of course, successful collaboration depends on a common, strongly felt commitment. So as traditional enterprises position themselves for a fight, they must understand how the competitive dynamics in their industries have shifted.

Increasing Returns to Scale Are Hard to Beat

Competitive advantage in many industries is moderated by decreasing returns to scale. In traditional product and service businesses, the value creation curve typically flattens out as the number of consumers increases, as we see in figure 1-2. A firm gains no particular advantage as its user base continues to increase beyond already efficient levels, which enables multiple competitors to coexist.

Some digital technologies, however, exhibit *increasing* returns to scale. A local advertising platform gets better and better as more and more users attract more and more ads. And as the number of ads increases, so does the ability to target the ads to the users, making individual ads more valuable. An advertising platform is thus similar to software platforms such as Windows, Linux, Android, and iOS, which exhibit increasing returns to scale—their growing value to consumers increases the number of available apps, while the value to app developers rises as the number of consumers rises. The more consumers, the greater the incentive for developers to build apps, and the more apps there are, the more motivated consumers are to use their digital devices.

FIGURE 1-2

Profiting from a growing customer base

For traditional product and service businesses, gaining additional customers does not continue adding commensurate value after a certain point. However, many platform businesses (Amazon, Facebook, and the like) become more and more valuable as more people and companies use them, connect with one another, and create network effects.

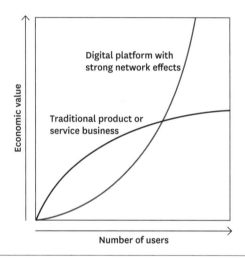

These considerations are important to the nature of hub competition. The economics of traditional decreasing returns make it possible for several competitors to coexist and provide differentiated value to attract users. That's the dynamic in the auto industry today, with many car manufacturers competing with one another to offer a variety of differentiated products. But the increasing returns in digital assets like ad platforms (or possibly driverless-car technology) will heighten the advantage of the competitor with the largest scale, the largest network of users, or the most data. And this is where the hub firms will most likely leverage their large and growing lead—and cause value to concentrate around them.

In contrast with traditional product and service businesses, network-based markets exhibiting increasing returns to scale will, over time, tip toward a narrow set of players. This implies that if a conventional decreasing-returns business (say, telecom or media) is threatened by a new type of competitor whose business model experiences increasing returns, the conventional player is in for a rough ride. With increasing returns to scale, a digital technology can provide a bottleneck to an entire industrial sector. And left alone, competitive bottlenecks dramatically skew value capture away from traditional firms.

Pushing Back

Hub firms often compete against one another. Microsoft has made substantial investments in augmented reality in an effort to create a new hub and counterbalance the power that Google and Apple wield in the mobile space.

Facebook acquired Oculus to force a similar structural shift in the emerging field of virtual reality. And a battle is looming in the smart-home arena, as Google, Apple, Microsoft, and Samsung attempt to reduce Amazon's early lead in voice-activated home technology.

But how does the rest of the economy deal with the increasing returns to scale of hub firms? With enough foresight and investment, traditional firms can resist by becoming hubs themselves, as we are seeing especially in the internet of things (IoT) space. GE is the classic example of this approach, with its investment in the Predix platform and the creation of GE Digital. Other companies are following suit in different settings—for example, Verizon and Vodafone with their IoT platforms.

Firms can also shape competition by investing to ensure that there are multiple hubs in each sector—and even influencing which ones win. They can organize to support less-established platforms, thus making a particular hub more viable and an industry sector more competitive in the long term. Deutsche Telekom, for instance, is partnering with Microsoft Azure (rather than Amazon Web Services) for cloud computing in Central Europe.

Most importantly, the value generated by networks will change as firms compete, innovate, and respond to community and regulatory pressure. Multihoming—a practice enabling participants on one hub's ecosystem to easily join another—can significantly mitigate the rise of hub power. For example, drivers and passengers routinely multihome across different ride-sharing platforms, often checking prices on Uber, Lyft, and Fasten to see which is offering the best deal. Retailers are starting to multihome across payment systems, supporting multiple solutions (such as Apple Pay, Google Wallet, and Samsung Pay). If multihoming is common, the market is less likely to tip to a single player, preserving competition and diffusing value capture. Indeed, companies will need to make their products and services available on multiple hubs and encourage the formation of new hubs to avoid being held hostage by one dominant player. Take the wireless-speaker manufacturer Sonos: It has ensured that its music system seamlessly integrates with as many music services as possible, including Apple Music, Amazon Music Unlimited, Google Play Music, Pandora, Spotify, and Tidal.

Collective action can also restructure economic networks, shape value creation and capture, and ease competitive bottlenecks. In the 1990s the open-source community organized to compete against Microsoft Windows with the Linux operating system. That effort was actively supported by traditional players such as IBM and Hewlett-Packard and reinforced later by Google and Facebook. Today Linux (and Linux-related products) are firmly established in enterprises, consumer devices, and cloud computing. Similarly, the Mozilla open-source community and its Firefox browser broke Microsoft's grip on navigating the internet. Even Apple, notorious for its proprietary approach, relies on open-source software for its core operating systems and web services, and the infamous iPhone jailbreaking craze demonstrated both the extraordinary demand for third-party apps and the burgeoning supply of them.

Open source has grown beyond all expectations to create an increasingly essential legacy of common intellectual property, capabilities, and methodologies. Now collective action is going well beyond code sharing to include coordination on data aggregation, the use of common infrastructure, and the standardization of practices to further equilibrate the power of hubs. Efforts like OpenStreetMap are leading the way in maps, and Mozilla's Common Voice project is crowdsourcing global voice data to open up the speech-recognition bottleneck.

Collective action will be increasingly crucial to sustaining balance in the digital economy. As economic sectors coalesce into networks and as powerful hubs continue to form, other stakeholders will need to work together to ensure that hubs look after the interests of all network members. Cooperation will become more important for the rivals that orbit hubs; indeed, strategic joint action by companies that are not hubs may be the best competitive antidote to the rising power of hub firms.

The public is also raising concerns about privacy, on-line tracking, cybersecurity, and data aggregation. Solutions being suggested include requirements for social network and data portability similar to the requirements for phone number portability that telecommunications regulators instituted to increase competition among phone service providers.

The Ethics of Network Leadership

The responsibility for sustaining our (digital) economy rests partly with the same leaders who are poised to control it. By developing such central positions of power and influence, hub firms have become de facto stewards of the long-term health of our economy. Leaders of hub companies need to realize that their organizations are analogous to "keystone" species in biological ecosystems—playing a critical role in maintaining their surroundings. Apple, Alibaba, Alphabet/Google, Amazon, and others that benefit disproportionately from the ecosystems they dominate have rational and ethical reasons to support the economic vitality of not just their direct participants but also the broader industries they serve. In particular, we argue that hub companies need to incorporate value sharing into their business models, along with value creation and value capture.

Building and maintaining a healthy ecosystem is in the best interests of hub companies. Amazon and Alibaba claim millions of marketplace sellers, and they profit from every transaction those merchants make. Similarly, Google and Apple earn billions in revenue from the third-party apps that run on their platforms. Both companies already invest heavily in the developer community, providing programming frameworks, software tools, and opportunities and business models that enable developers to grow their businesses. But such efforts will need to be scaled up and refined as hub firms find themselves at the center of—and relying on—much larger and more-complex ecosystems. Preserving the strength and productivity of complementary communities should be a fundamental part of any hub firm's strategy.

Uber provides an interesting example of the repercussions of getting this wrong. Uber's viability depends on its relations with its drivers and riders, who have often criticized the company's practices. Under pressure from those communities—and from competitors that offer drivers the potential to earn more—Uber is making improvements. Still, its challenges suggest that no hub will maintain an advantage over the long term if it neglects the well-being of its ecosystem partners. Microsoft learned a hard lesson when it failed to maintain the health of its PC software ecosystem, losing out to the Linux community in cloud services. But network ethics are not just about financial considerations. Social concerns are equally important. Centralized platforms, such as Kiva for charitable impact investing and Airbnb for accommodation bookings, have been found to be susceptible to racial discrimination. In Airbnb's case, external researchers convincingly demonstrated that African American guests were especially likely to have their reservation requests rejected. The pressure is now on Airbnb to fight bias both by educating its proprietors and by modifying certain platform features. Additionally, as Airbnb continues to grow, it must work to ensure that its hosts heed municipal regulations, lest they face a potentially devastating regulatory backlash.

Indeed, if hubs do not promote the health and sustainability of the many firms and individuals in their networks, other forces will undoubtedly step in. Governments and regulators will increasingly act to encourage competition, protect consumer welfare, and foster economic stability. Consider the challenges Google faces in Europe, where regulators are concerned about the dominance of both its search advertising business and its Android platform.

The centralizing forces of digitization are not going to slow down anytime soon. The emergence of powerful hub firms is well underway, and the threats to global economic well-being are unmistakable. All actors in the economy—but particularly the hub firms themselves—should work to sustain the entire ecosystem and observe new principles, for both strategic and ethical reasons. Otherwise, we are all in serious trouble.

TAKEAWAYS

A small number of digital superpowers have become "hub firms" that control access to billions of mobile customers coveted by all kinds of product and service providers. These hubs drive increasing returns to scale and claim a disproportionate share of the value being created in the global economy.

- ✓ The hub economy will continue to spread across more industries, concentrating more power in the hands of a few.

- ✓ As hubs proliferate and expand their reach, they will exacerbate economic inequality and threaten social stability. All stakeholders—traditional companies, startups, institutions, and communities—will need to change the way they do business.

✓ Hub firms themselves must lead responsibly for the good of all, not just creating and capturing value but doing more to sustain other players in the ecosystem.

Adapted from an article in Harvard Business Review, *September–October 2017 (product #R1705F).*

2

IS LACK OF COMPETITION STRANGLING THE U.S. ECONOMY?

by David Wessel

Despite their undeniable popularity, Apple, Amazon, Google, and Facebook are drawing increasing scrutiny from economists, legal scholars, politicians, and policy wonks, who accuse these firms of using their size and strength to crush potential competitors. (Their clout caught the attention of European regulators long ago.) The tech giants pose unique challenges, but they also represent just one piece of a broader story: a troubling phenomenon of too little competition throughout the U.S. economy.

There's no question that most industries are becoming more concentrated. Big firms account for higher shares of industry revenue and are reaping historically large profits relative to their investment. This is not necessarily a bad thing. As an all-star quintet of economists—David Autor, David Dorn, Lawrence Katz, Christina Patterson, and John Van Reenen—points out, concentration and higher profits can be benign, perhaps even welcome, consequences of technological innovation. We now operate in a winner-take-most world, the argument goes, in which superstar firms with higher productivity capture a larger slice of the market; Amazon, Apple, Facebook, and Google have risen to the top because of their propensity to innovate. According to James Bessen of Boston University, the increasing share of revenue captured by the top firms in industries outside of high tech is explained by those firms' adoption of proprietary, mission-critical information technology: They're bigger because they're better.

Mounting evidence, however, strongly suggests that harmful forces are also at play. "Concentration could arise from anticompetitive forces," Autor and his colleagues note, "whereby dominant firms are increasingly able to prevent actual and potential rivals from entering and expanding." Indeed, research shows that incumbent firms in a wide range of industries—airlines, beer, pharmaceuticals, hospitals—are wielding market power in ways that prevent rivals from emerging and thriving. The winners are winning bigger, while the number of new startups is falling. With waning competitive pressure, productivity growth slows, wages stagnate, and the gap between winners and losers widens.

The underlying problem is not "bigness" per se. Rather, it's the combined effect of size, concentration, and, importantly, incumbent-friendly regulation on the healthy competition that propels economic growth. In this article, I examine the troubling effect of industry consolidation on competition. I then look at the role of antitrust law and regulation in shaping today's economic environment and explore strategies to improve the flow of innovation, enhance dynamism in business and in labor markets, and ultimately deliver higher standards of living for all.

The Warning Signs

Ten years ago, the top four U.S. airlines collected 41% of the industry's revenue. Today, they collect 65%. Although competition is stiff on the most heavily traveled air routes, 97% of routes between pairs of cities have so few competitors that standard antitrust metrics would deem them "highly concentrated." In 1990, 65% of hospitals in metropolitan areas were "highly concentrated." By 2016, 90% were. It's a similar story in the beer business. Despite the proliferation of craft breweries, four brewers hold nearly 90% of the U.S. beer market.

These are not isolated cases. In a 2002 study, Lawrence White, a New York University economist, concluded that economy-wide concentration had fallen from the beginning of the 1980s to the end of the 1990s. When he took another look, in 2017, the story had changed. With scholarly caution, he noted "a moderate but continued increase in aggregate concentration." The *Economist*, using U.S. Economic Census data, found a similar trend. Of the 893 industries it examined—from dog food and battery makers to airlines and credit cards—two-thirds had grown more concentrated since 2007. Weighted by size of industry, the top four firms' share of revenue had risen to 32% in 2012 from 26% in 1997.

Clearly, industry concentration is on the rise. But does that mean there is less competition or that consumers are worse off? The best way to discern if increasing concentration is worrisome economically is to look at profits, investment, business dynamism, and prices. In most (though not all) cases, the data points to a lack of competition.

Profits

High and rising profits in an increasingly concentrated market are typically a sign of lessening competition and increased market power by dominant firms. Today, profits are up in industries in which a shrinking number of players have a growing share of the business. Recent research suggests that the average markup—the difference between the prices firms charge and products' marginal cost—is rising in American business, and rising fastest for the most profitable firms. Using data for all publicly traded U.S. firms from 1950 to 2014, Jan De Loecker of Princeton and Jan Eeckhout of University College London found that markups rose from about 18% in 1980 to 67% in 2014. That's good for shareholders, of course, but it's not so good for consumers or the overall economy.

Investment

Another signal of declining competitive pressure is firms' ability to increase profits without much investment; in competitive markets, companies are driven to invest more to stay ahead of their rivals. Business investment across the economy has perked up lately, but it is not as robust as one might expect given the surge in profits, the extraordinarily low cost of equity and debt, and the amount of cash on corporate balance sheets. Measured against GDP, corporate after-tax profits are almost double what they were 25 years ago—and higher than at any time since World War II—yet business investment as a share of GDP is up only 13% over the same period. "Investment is weak relative to profitability and valuation," NYU's Thomas Philippon and German Gutierrez concluded in a 2017 analysis built on the historical relationship between investment and the ratio of the market value of a company's debt and equity to the replacement cost of its assets.

Business dynamism

In a healthy economy, companies continually are born, fail, expand, and contract, while new jobs are created and others are destroyed. A slowdown in business dynamism means that entrenched firms have less to fear from upstarts; as a result, the economy suffers as innovation slows and job growth stalls. In the United States, the rate of birth of new firms (as a percentage of all firms) fell from above 13% in the late 1980s to around 8% in 2015, according to the most recent official data. The number of jobs created by businesses less than a year old dropped from a peak of 4.7 million in the late 1990s to 3 million in 2015.

John Haltiwanger, a University of Maryland economist, notes that the decline in dynamism in the United States originated in the retail sector in the 1980s and 1990s. But even as the number of retailers starting up and dying off plunged, the industry became more productive. This was dubbed "the Walmart effect," because of the impact of the giant retailer not only on the efficiency of its industry but on the entire U.S. economy. Lately, though, declining dynamism has spread to the tech sector. That's more worrisome, Haltiwanger says, because it portends slower productivity growth.

Prices

Economic theory suggests that oligopolies—industries in which a few firms dominate without much competition—lead to increases in price and reductions in output. In determining whether competition is on the decline, a review of prices by some researchers yields an inconclusive result.

Sharat Ganapati of Dartmouth, for instance, looks at data from 1972 to 2012 and concludes that increased concentration in manufacturing is correlated with higher prices, which is consistent with declining competition, but also with stable output, which is not. Outside of manufacturing, industry concentration is correlated with higher output and stable prices, neither of which conforms to the theory of oligopoly and declining competition.

The preponderance of evidence across the proliferating body of research suggests that industry consolidation is causing a troubling decline in competition, limiting the country's capacity to innovate, create jobs, and sustain overall economic health.

Heroes or Villains?

Despite an overall picture of declining competition, it's not always easy to determine whether or to what extent consumers in a particular industry are harmed by consolidation. Are companies that rise to the top "heroes" or "villains"?

Consider Facebook and its 2017 acquisition of TBH (for "To Be Honest"), a mobile app popular with teenagers that allows them to anonymously answer questions about their friends. When Facebook snapped it up, the app was only two months old but had attracted more than 5 million users and logged more than a billion sent messages. TBH is only one of more than 60 such acquisitions by Facebook since 2010.

Seen through the hero lens, the prospect of selling out to Facebook (or Google or Apple) offers many economic advantages. The promise of a generous payout is a huge incentive to innovative entrepreneurs. On a broader scale, the capacity of Facebook's platform to spread innovation throughout the economy means that benefits from technological advances accrue faster and more broadly than they would in the hands of a startup. Seen through the villain lens, however, Facebook's relentless swallowing up of promising young firms effectively squashes the potential of upstarts to become competitors. We'll never know what TBH or Halli Labs or Orbitera or Instagram or WhatsApp or Oculus VR might have become had Facebook not absorbed them—or what companies might have been started had prospective founders not figured that it would be impossible to compete with Facebook.

In some industries, concentration clearly is driven less by innovative superstars than by anticompetitive behavior. Consider beer. Despite the proliferation of craft breweries, two producers dominate the U.S. market: Anheuser-Busch InBev (Beck's, Budweiser, Corona, Michelob, Stella Artois) and MillerCoors (Blue Moon, Coors, Miller,

Molson). Recent research pins rising beer prices to greater concentration in the industry. When SABMiller and MolsonCoors (the number two and three brewers at the time) combined U.S. operations, in 2008, prices abruptly rose—and not only for their beers but also for those of competitor Anheuser-Busch. Economists Nathan Miller of Georgetown and Matthew Weinberg of Drexel estimated that prices were at least 6% and 8% higher than they would have been without the joint venture and suggested that the competing brewers coordinated pricing. In 2015, the Justice Department, citing corporate documents in its initial objection to a subsequent Anheuser-Busch acquisition, said the brewer's strategic plan for pricing "reads like a how-to manual for successful price coordination."

Health care is another stark example. A wave of hospital mergers and consolidations across the country, driven in part by a push for better coordination of care and greater efficiency, has strengthened hospitals' bargaining power relative to insurers' without much sign of the hoped-for benefits in productivity. "Although provider concentration could produce efficiencies that benefit purchasers of health care services, the evidence does not point in that direction," Berkeley's Brent Fulton concludes in a 2017 review of the literature. Concentration in hospital markets is also associated with higher prices, with surges of up to 20% following mergers. A 2010 analysis found that the typical private-insurer payment for inpatient hospital stays in San Francisco (a highly concentrated market) was about 75% higher than in the more fragmented Los Angeles market.

So are industry leaders heroes or villains? Probably a bit of both. "Most firms are actively engaged in protecting their source of competitive advantage through a mixture of innovation, lobbying, or both," says Luigi Zingales of the University of Chicago. To the extent that firms are being driven to innovate, there is little to worry about. But when corporations use their market power to shape the policy and regulatory environment in ways that crush competition, problems arise. And unfortunately, there's more than enough evidence to conclude that a substantial portion of the U.S. economy suffers from a lack of competition.

Reshaping the Antitrust Framework

In remedying the harmful effects of industry consolidation and declining competition, an obvious place to start is antitrust regulation and enforcement. The U.S. approach to antitrust has evolved significantly over the past century. In the 1950s and 1960s, many mergers—even ones that would have led to relatively modest increases in concentration—were routinely challenged, but in the 1970s the antitrust framework began to shift toward challenging many fewer mergers. Lawyer-judges Robert Bork and Richard Posner and Nobel laureate economists George Stigler and Oliver Williamson laid the intellectual foundation for this shift, which spread to the policy arena and the courts in the early 1980s.

The more lenient approach relied on three ideas: that harm from increased concentration had to be weighed against the efficiencies to be achieved, that horizontal mergers between competitors were harmful only if they led to less output, and that vertical mergers between supplier and buyer generally were not a problem. This thinking solidified under the Reagan Justice Department, and for better or worse, the antitrust authorities stood by over the coming decades as the economy grew more concentrated. In the 2000s, under Barack Obama, the stance became somewhat more aggressive, but it remains unclear whether his executive orders to promote competitive markets, issued in the closing innings of his administration, were mere symbolism or a serious effort.

It is time for antitrust authorities to renew their scrutiny of traditional mergers. A comprehensive review of retrospective studies of the thousands of mergers and joint ventures over the past 25 years by Northeastern

University economist John Kwoka judged that antitrust authorities had been too tolerant both in letting certain types of mergers go unchallenged and in imposing conditions on mergers that were cleared. Prices following a subset of these mergers rose by an average of 4.3%, holding other factors constant, Kwoka found. The increases were particularly large in the airline and health care industries. "The diminished attention to mergers involving somewhat lower market shares and concentration appears to have resulted in approval of significantly more mergers that prove to be anticompetitive," he wrote in a 2015 book.

Kwoka's meta-analysis suggests that antitrust authorities should be more inclined to block mergers in order to increase competition. Consider the wireless telephone business. In 2011, AT&T sought to acquire a struggling competitor, T-Mobile USA, in a $39 billion deal that would have reduced the number of major competitors in the industry from four to three. Unable to overcome the opposition of the Obama administration, however, AT&T abandoned the deal five months after announcing it. After the merger fell through, some argued that T-Mobile was doomed. It wasn't. As writer Mark Rogowsky recounted in *Forbes*, "Within a year, T-Mobile hired John Legere as its new CEO and he threw out the business-as-usual approach. Legere dumped subsidies, lowered prices, offered more data and often poked fun at rivals." T-Mobile thrived, signing up 4.4 million new subscribers in 2013. By 2017, competition among wireless carriers was so stiff that Federal Reserve chair Janet Yellen cited falling prices for cell phone service as a cause of low inflation.

Antitrust authorities must also tackle the vexing question of what constitutes illegal "predatory" pricing in today's market. Consider Amazon's alleged use of below-cost pricing to pressure and ultimately acquire a potential competitor. After the e-commerce company Quidsi—the owner of Diapers.com—rejected a 2009 acquisition overture from Amazon, Amazon responded by cutting prices for diapers and other baby products by as much as 30% on its site and rolling out Amazon Mom, which offered discounts and free shipping. Quidsi struggled, flirted with Walmart, but eventually sold itself to Amazon. By 2012, Amazon had begun raising prices and had slashed the benefits of Amazon Mom.

These are live issues. In 2015, for instance, the Federal Trade Commission considered whether the merger of real estate sites Zillow and Trulia would reduce both companies' incentives to develop new features for consumers. The FTC decided that it wouldn't, and the merger went through. But in the same year, FTC sought to block a merger between Steris and Synergy Health, the number two and three companies in the health care facility-sterilization business. Because Synergy didn't do business in the United States at the time, the FTC argued, a merger would preclude any competition that might result from Synergy's eventual entrance into the U.S. market. A federal judge disagreed, and the merger was consummated.

Even-more-complicated issues will arise as the economy evolves. How should the authorities view the unprecedented power of the new digital giants to crush competitors? Should they be more skeptical about mergers that might lessen "potential competition," which occurs when one firm buys another in an adjacent market (think Google's acquisition of YouTube or Microsoft's acquisition of LinkedIn)? How about when a big firm swallows a tiny firm that might have grown into a mighty oak?

The argument for reexamining current merger guidelines—and, where appropriate, challenging the case law that is said to make Department of Justice and FTC lawyers reluctant to bring cases—is very strong. The economy is more concentrated. Evidence that there's too little competition is accumulating. Acquisitions that in the past were too small to attract the usual antitrust scrutiny can eliminate potential competition, especially in a world where a company like WhatsApp can grow in just a few years to reach a billion users a day. Indeed, the power of new tech giants to use their potent networks and the vast amounts of data they collect to thwart competition is one of the biggest challenges facing antitrust authorities today.

Rethinking Regulation

The worrisome aspects of increasing industry consolidation can't be addressed solely through antitrust enforcement. Policy makers also need to scrutinize regulations that restrict competition across the economy. Owing in part to incumbent firms' influence in shaping policy to preserve their positions at the expense of startups and other would-be competitors, the United States is no longer held up as an exemplar of free markets and regulatory restraint. In fact, in a dramatic change from the late 1990s, the Organization for Economic Cooperation and Development says the U.S. now regulates product markets more heavily than many developed economies including Australia, Canada, France, Germany, and Japan.

Take the pharmaceutical industry. Although the United States doesn't regulate pharmaceutical prices, as most rich countries do, it offers makers of brand-name drugs patent protection, periods of exclusivity, and other ways to recoup their investment in expensive research that produces new drugs. Once those protections expire, however, prices theoretically should fall as makers of generics enter the market. And that does happen—sometimes.

According to Yale economist Fiona Scott Morton, however, over the past 10 to 15 years "industry participants have managed to disable many of these competitive mechanisms and create niches in which drugs can be sold with little to no competition." For example, the marketing of some drugs with particularly severe side effects is now very tightly controlled through the FDA's Risk Evaluation and Mitigation Strategy, or REMS. The makers of those drugs, in some instances, cite the restrictions as a reason not to supply a generic maker with a sample to re-create the drugs. For example, it took Hikma Pharmaceuticals nearly seven years of litigation to get what it needed to produce, in accordance with REMS restrictions, a generic version of Jazz Pharmaceuticals' major product, Xyrem, a $1-billion-a-year drug used to treat narcolepsy. The 2017 settlement allows Hikma to begin marketing the generic version only after January 1, 2023. Early in his tenure as President Trump's FDA commissioner, Scott Gottlieb vowed to change the REMS rules to prevent drugmakers from using them to thwart generic competition and in 2018 announced a preliminary plan to do so.

Regulations in the labor market, along with certain employer practices, can also conspire to constrain competition, by limiting workers' ability to seek new or higher-paying jobs. As the famed economist Adam Smith warned, corporations continue to behave in ways that seek "always and everywhere in a sort of tacit, but constant and uniform combination, not to raise the wages of labor." One way companies do this is by requiring workers to sign noncompete agreements. When enforced, these agreements inhibit a worker's ability to switch jobs and constrain the ability of new firms to hire talent. Software engineers and CEOs are not the only ones affected by such regulations: Among employees earning $40,000 or less, about one in seven (13.5%) is bound by a noncompete. In an eyebrow-raising 2017 study, Princeton's Alan Krueger and Orley Ashenfelter found that 58% of major chains (Burger King, Jiffy Lube, H&R Block, and dozens more) restrict and sometimes prohibit one franchisee from hiring workers away from another, to the obvious detriment of people seeking to change jobs.

The explosion of state occupational licensing rules also harms both workers and new entrants. In the 1960s, only 10% of U.S. workers had an occupational license. At last count, 22% do. Much of the increase is a result of states extending the occupations for which licenses are required. Some of the requirements are motivated by an urge to protect consumers, but others were clearly orchestrated through lobbying from trade associations eager to raise barriers to entry, limit the number of players in their profession, and raise prices. Louisiana requires florists to be licensed. Michigan requires 1,460 days of training for athletic trainers, but only 26 days for emergency medical technicians. California's Board of Barbering and Cosmetology requires 1,600 hours of education and hands-on training before a person can take the licensing exam, and another 3,200 hours of apprenticeship and 220 hours of related training are required for licensure. States generally don't recognize credentials issued by other states, making it hard for licensed workers to move across state lines and protecting existing license holders in any state.

Such regulatory restraints on competition are coming under increasing scrutiny. The Federal Trade Commission has been in a long-running battle with dentists' organizations over various state rules that limit the services hygienists and teeth-whitening clinics can offer. Creating a category of "dental therapists" to provide some routine services "could benefit consumers by increasing choice, competition and access to care, especially for the underserved," the FTC said. The dentists are not happy.

In 2014, under pressure from the Federal Communications Commission, the wireless phone industry finally agreed to allow consumers to unlock their cell phones if they wanted to change providers. And with bipartisan enthusiasm and the blessing of the Food and Drug Administration, Congress in 2017 instructed the FDA to make it easier for consumers to buy hearing aids at Costco and other retailers, just as they can buy reading glasses at nonspecialty stores such as CVS. The notion was to spur competition and lower prices, discouraging the practice of some audiologists of bundling an exam with the purchase of a hearing aid.

This is a start, but regulators and policy makers have more work to do.

The Way Forward

Ultimately, curing what ails the U.S. economy requires political commitment and resolve to protect the robust competition that spurs productivity growth and improves American living standards, even when well-resourced interests resist.

If we're slow to take action to bolster competition—perhaps because incumbents successfully wield their power or because of a distaste for regulation of any sort—we risk diluting the dynamism of the economy and restricting the flow of innovations and new ideas, darkening the prospects for our children and grandchildren.

TAKEAWAYS

Tech giants are drawing increasing scrutiny from economists, legal scholars, politicians, and policy wonks, who accuse these firms of using their size and strength to crush potential competitors.

✓ Economists are trying to understand whether the concentration of U.S. industries is bad for competition. Their findings point in many different directions—innovation superstars like Google have created winner-take-most markets largely by exploiting network effects, not through predatory behavior. Yet research from the wider economy uncovers classic signs of unhealthy concentration: rising profits, weak investment, and low business dynamism.

✓ The U.S. approach to antitrust has evolved significantly; in the 1950s and 1960s, many mergers—even ones that would have led to relatively modest increases in industry concentration—were routinely challenged. Since the 1970s, however, the antitrust framework has shifted toward challenging many fewer mergers.

✓ Regulators need to pay greater attention to protecting economic vitality and consumer well-being. It is time for another overhaul of antitrust regulations.

Adapted from an article in Harvard Business Review, *March–April 2018 (product #R1802H).*

Section 2

THE FUTURE OF ANTITRUST AND REGULATION

3

WHY IT'S A BAD IDEA TO LET A FEW TECH COMPANIES MONOPOLIZE OUR DATA

by Maurice E. Stucke

t's no good fighting an election campaign on the facts," Cambridge Analytica's managing director told an undercover reporter, "because actually it's all about emotion."[1] To target U.S. voters and appeal to their hopes, neuroses, and fears, the political consulting firm needed to train its algorithm to predict and map personality traits. That required lots of personal data. So, to build these psychographic profiles, Cambridge Analytica enlisted a Cambridge University professor, whose app collected data on about 50 million Facebook users and their friends. Facebook, at that time, allowed app developers to collect this personal data. Facebook argued that Cambridge Analytica and the professor violated its data policies. But this was not the first time its policies were violated. Nor is it likely to be the last.

This scandal came on the heels of Russia using Facebook, Google, and Twitter "to sow discord in the U.S. political system, including the 2016 U.S. presidential election." It heightened concerns over today's tech giants and the influence they have.

That influence comes in part from data. Facebook, Google, Amazon, and similar companies are "dataopolies." By that I mean companies that control a key platform, which, like a coral reef, attracts to its ecosystem users, sellers, advertisers, software developers, apps, and accessory makers. Apple and Google, for example, each control a popular mobile phone operating system platform (and key apps on that platform), Amazon controls the largest online merchant platform, and Facebook controls the largest social network platform. Through their leading platforms, a significant *volume* and *variety* of personal data flow. The *velocity* in acquiring and exploiting this personal data can help these companies obtain significant market power.

Is it OK for a few firms to possess so much data and thereby wield so much power? In the United States, at least, antitrust officials so far seem ambivalent about these data-opolies. They're free, the thinking goes, so what's the harm? But that reasoning is misguided. Data-opolies pose tremendous risks, for consumers, workers, competition, and the overall health of our democracy. Here's why.

Why U.S. Antitrust Isn't Worried About Data-opolies

The European competition authorities have recently brought actions against four data-opolies: Google, Apple, Facebook, and Amazon (or GAFA for short). The European Commission, for example, fined Google a record €2.42 billion for leveraging its monopoly in search to advance its comparative shopping service. The commission also preliminarily found Google to have abused its dominant position both with its Android mobile operating system and with AdSense. Facebook, Germany's competition agency preliminarily found, abused its dominant position "by making the use of its social network conditional on its being allowed to limitlessly amass every kind of data generated by using third-party websites and merge it with the user's Facebook account."

We will likely see more fines and other remedies in the next few years from the Europeans. But in the United States, the data-opolies largely escaped antitrust scrutiny under both the Obama and Bush administrations. Notably, while the European Commission found Google's search bias to be anticompetitive, the U.S. Federal Trade Commission did not. From 2000 until 2017, the Department of Justice brought only one monopolization case in total, against anyone. (In contrast, the DOJ, between 1970 and 1972, brought 39 civil and 3 criminal cases against monopolies and oligopolies.)

The head of the DOJ's Antitrust Division recognized the enforcement gap between the United States and Europe. He noted his agency's "particular concerns in digital markets." But absent "demonstrable harm to competition and consumers," the DOJ is "reluctant to impose special duties on digital platforms, out of [its] concern that special duties might stifle the very innovation that has created dynamic competition for the benefit of consumers."[2]

So, the divergence in antitrust enforcement may reflect differences over these data-opolies' perceived harms. Ordinarily the harm from monopolies is higher prices, less output, or reduced quality. It superficially appears that data-opolies pose little, if any, risk of these harms. Unlike some pharmaceuticals, data-opolies do not charge consumers exorbitant prices. Most of Google's and Facebook's consumer products are ostensibly "free." The data-opolies' scale can also mean higher-quality products. The more people use a particular search engine, the more the search engine's algorithm can learn users' preferences, the more relevant the search results will likely be, which in turn will likely attract others to the search engine, and the positive feedback continues.

As Robert Bork argued, there "is no coherent case for monopolization because a search engine, like Google, is free to consumers and they can switch to an alternative search engine with a click."[3]

How Data-opolies Harm

But higher prices are not the only way for powerful companies to harm their consumers or the rest of society. Upon closer examination, data-opolies can pose at least eight potential harms.

Lower-quality products with less privacy

Companies, antitrust authorities increasingly recognize, can compete on privacy and protecting data. But without competition, data-opolies face less pressure. They can depress privacy protection *below* competitive levels and collect personal data *above* competitive levels. The collection of too much personal data can be the equivalent of charging an excessive price.

Data-opolies can also fail to disclose *what* data they collect and *how* they will use the data. They face little competitive pressure to change their opaque privacy policies. Even if a data-opoly improves its privacy statement, so what? The current notice-and-consent regime is meaningless when there are no viable competitive alternatives and the bargaining power is so unequal.

Surveillance and security risks

In a monopolized market, personal data is concentrated in a few firms. Consumers have limited outside options that offer better privacy protection. This raises additional risks, including:

- **Government capture.** The fewer the number of firms controlling the personal data, the greater the potential risk that a government will "capture" the firm. Companies need things from government; governments often want access to data. When there are only a few firms, this can increase the likelihood of companies secretly cooperating with the government to provide access to data. China, for example, relies on its data-opolies to better monitor its population.

- **Covert surveillance.** Even if the government cannot capture a data-opoly, its rich data trove increases a government's incentive to circumvent the data-opoly's privacy protections to tap into the personal data. Even if the government can't strike a deal to access the data directly, it may be able to do so covertly.

- **Implications of a data policy violation/security breach.** Data-opolies have greater incentives to prevent a breach than do typical firms. But with more personal data concentrated in fewer companies, hackers, marketers, and political consultants, among others, have even greater incentives to find ways to circumvent or breach the dominant firm's security measures. The concentration of data means that if one of them is breached, the harm done could be orders of magnitude greater than with a normal company. While consumers may be outraged, a dominant firm has less reason to worry that consumers are switching to rivals.

Wealth transfer to data-opolies

Even when their products and services are ostensibly "free," data-opolies can extract significant wealth in several ways that they otherwise couldn't in a competitive market.

First, data-opolies can extract wealth by getting personal data without having to pay for the data's fair market value. The personal data collected may be worth far more than the cost of providing the free service. The fact that the service is free does not mean we are fairly compensated for our data. Thus, data-opolies have a strong economic incentive to maintain the status quo, in which users, as the *MIT Technology Review* put it, "have little idea how much personal data they have provided, how it is used, and what it is worth."[4] If the public knew, and if they had viable alternatives, they might hold out for compensation.

Second, something similar can happen with the content users create. Data-opolies can extract wealth by getting creative content from users for free. In a competitive market, users could conceivably demand compensation not only for their data but also for their contributions to YouTube and Facebook. With no viable alternatives, they cannot.

Third, data-opolies can extract wealth from sellers upstream. One example is when data-opolies scrape valuable content from photographers, authors, musicians, and other websites and post it on their own platform. In this case, the wealth of the data-opolies comes at the expense of other businesses in their value chain.

Fourth, data-opolies can extract our wealth indirectly, when their higher advertising fees are passed along in the prices for the advertised goods and services. If the data-opolies faced more competitors for their advertising services, ads could cost even less—and therefore so might the products being advertised.

Finally, data-opolies can extract wealth from both sellers upstream and consumers downstream by facilitating or engaging in "behavioral discrimination," a form of price discrimination based on past behavior—like, say, your internet browsing. They can use the personal data to get people to buy things they did not necessarily want at the highest price they are willing to pay.

As data-opolies expand their platforms to digital personal assistants, the internet of things, and smart technologies, the concern is that their data advantage will increase their competitive advantage and market power. As a result, the data-opolies' monopoly profits will likely increase, at our expense.

Loss of trust

Market economies rely on trust. For online markets to deliver their benefits, people must trust firms and their use of the personal data. But as technology evolves and more personal data is collected, we are increasingly aware that a few powerful firms are using our personal information for their own benefit, not ours. When data-opolies degrade privacy protections below competitive levels, some consumers will choose not "to share their data, to limit their data sharing with companies, or even to lie when providing information," as the UK's Competition and Markets Authority put it. Consumers may forgo the data-opolies' services, which they otherwise would have used if privacy competition were robust. This loss would represent what economists call a deadweight welfare loss. In other words, as distrust increases, society overall becomes worse off.

Significant costs on third parties

Additionally, data-opolies that control a key platform, like a mobile phone operating system, can cheaply exclude rivals by:

- Steering users and advertisers to their own products and services to the detriment of rival sellers on the platform (and contrary to consumers' wishes)

- Degrading an independent app's functionality

- Reducing traffic to an independent app by making it harder to find on its search engine or app store

Data-opolies can also impose costs on companies seeking to protect our privacy interests. My book with Ariel Ezrachi, *Virtual Competition*, discusses the example of Google kicking the privacy app Disconnect out of its Android app store.

Less innovation in markets dominated by data-opolies

Data-opolies can chill innovation with a weapon that earlier monopolies lacked. Allen Grunes and I call it the "now-casting radar." Our book *Big Data and Competition Policy* explores how some platforms have a relative advantage in accessing and analyzing data to discern consumer trends well before others. Data-opolies can use their relative advantage to see what products or services are becoming more popular. With their now-casting radar, data-opolies can acquire or squelch these nascent competitive threats.

Social and moral concerns

Historically, antitrust has also been concerned with how monopolies can hinder individual autonomy. Data-opolies can also hurt individual autonomy. To start with, they can direct (and limit) opportunities for startups that subsist on their super-platform. This includes third-party sellers that rely on Amazon's platform to reach consumers, newspapers, and journalists that depend on Facebook and Google to reach younger readers, and, as the European Commission's Google Shopping Case explores, companies that depend on traffic from Google's search engine.

But the autonomy concerns go beyond the constellation of app developers, sellers, journalists, musicians, writers, photographers, and artists dependent on the data-opoly to reach users. Every individual's autonomy is at stake.

In 2018, the hedge fund Jana Partners joined the California State Teachers' Retirement pension fund to demand that Apple do more to address the effects of its devices on children. As the *Economist* noted, "You know you are in trouble if a Wall Street firm is lecturing you about morality."[5] The concern is that the data-opolies' products are purposefully addictive and thereby eroding individuals' ability to make free choices.

An interesting counterargument worth noting is based on the interplay between monopoly power and competition. On the one hand, in monopolized markets, consumers have fewer competitive options. So, arguably, there is less need to addict them. On the other hand, data-opolies, like Facebook and Google, even without significant rivals, can increase profits by increasing our engagement with their products. So, data-opolies can have an incentive to exploit behavioral biases and imperfect willpower to addict users—whether watching YouTube videos or posting on Instagram.

Political concerns

Economic power often translates into political power. Unlike earlier monopolies, data-opolies, given how they interact with individuals, possess a more powerful tool:

namely, the ability to affect the public debate and our perception of right and wrong.

Many people now receive their news from social media platforms. But the news isn't just passively transmitted. Data-opolies can affect how we feel and think. Facebook, for example, in an "emotional contagion" study, manipulated 689,003 users' emotions by altering their news feed. Other risks of this sort include:[6]

- **Bias.** In filtering the information we receive based on our preferences, data-opolies can reduce the viewpoints we receive, thereby leading to "echo chambers" and "filter bubbles."

- **Censorship.** Data-opolies, through their platform, can control or block content that users receive, and enforce governmental censorship of political or religious information.

- **Manipulation.** Data-opolies can promote stories that further their particular business or political interests, instead of their relevance or quality.

Limiting the Power of Data-opolies

Upon closer examination, data-opolies can actually be *more* dangerous than traditional monopolies. They can affect not only our wallets but our privacy, autonomy, democracy, and well-being.

Markets dominated by these data-opolies will not necessarily self-correct. Network effects, high switching costs for consumers (given the lack of data portability and user rights over their data), and weak privacy protection help data-opolies maintain their dominance.

Luckily, global antitrust enforcement can help. The Reagan administration, in espousing the then-popular Chicago school of economic thought, discounted concerns about monopolies. The Supreme Court, relying on faulty economic reasoning, surmised that charging monopoly prices was "an important element of the free market system." With the rise of the progressive, antimonopoly New Brandeis school, the pendulum is swinging the other way. Given the emergence of data-opolies, this is a welcome change.

Nonetheless, global antitrust enforcement, while a necessary tool to deter these harms, is not sufficient. Antitrust enforcers must coordinate with privacy and consumer protection officials to ensure that the conditions for effective privacy competition and an inclusive economy are in place.

Many tech giants are "data-opolies." The volume, variety, and velocity of personal data flows through these ecosystems help these companies gain significant market power. They control key platforms that attract users, sellers, advertisers, software developers, apps, and accessory makers to their ecosystems.

✓ Data-opolies may actually be *more* dangerous than traditional monopolies. They can affect not only consumers' wallets but their privacy, autonomy, democracy, and well-being.

✓ While European competition authorities have recently brought actions against four data-opolies, those tech companies have so far escaped antitrust scrutiny in the United States.

✓ Allowing data-opolies to go unchecked introduces a number of potential harms including security risks, declining innovation, and social, moral, and political concerns.

NOTES

1. David A. Graham, "Not Even Cambridge Analytica Believed Its Hype," *Atlantic*, March 20, 2018, https://www.theatlantic.com /politics/archive/2018/03/cambridge-analyticas-self-own/556016/.

2. U.S. Department of Justice, "Assistant Attorney General Makan Delrahim Delivers Remarks at the College of Europe in Brussels," press release, February 21, 2018, https://www.justice.gov /opa/speech/assistant-attorney-general-makan-delrahim-delivers -remarks-college-europe-brussels.

3. Robert H. Bork, "Antitrust and Google," *Chicago Tribune*, April 6, 2012, https://www.chicagotribune.com/opinion/ct-xpm -2012-04-06-ct-perspec-0405-bork-20120406-story.html.

4. Tom Simonite, "If Facebook Can Profit from Your Data, Why Can't You?" *MIT Technology Review,* July 30, 2013, https://www .technologyreview.com/s/517356/if-facebook-can-profit-from-your -data-why-cant-you/.

5. Eve Smith, "The Techlash Against Amazon, Facebook and Google—and What They Can Do," *Economist*, January 20, 2018, https://www.economist.com/briefing/2018/01/20/the-techlash -against-amazon-facebook-and-google-and-what-they-can-do.

6. Adam D. I. Kramer, Jamie E. Guillory, and Jeffrey T. Hancock, "Experimental Evidence of Massive-Scale Emotional Contagion Through Social Networks," *PNAS* 24, no. 111 (June 2, 2014).

Adapted from "Here Are All the Reasons It's a Bad Idea to Let a Few Tech Companies Monopolize Our Data," on hbr.org, March 27, 2018 (product #H048R4).

WHAT THE FUTURE OF U.S. ANTITRUST SHOULD LOOK LIKE

by William A. Galston and Clara Hendrickson

Market concentration is rising while economic competition—the bedrock of a dynamic, free market economy—is under threat. No wonder the framework that has guided antitrust enforcement for the last four decades is coming under intense scrutiny.

There are at least three schools of thought about the future of antitrust, each of which deserves consideration. To determine which one is best—and we do have a view—it's helpful to review the growing evidence on why market concentration is so dangerous to the economy.

The Perils of Industry Concentration

A comprehensive study of recent mergers found that product prices rose postmerger in nearly two-thirds of cases. Price increases are particularly burdensome for individuals and families on the lower end of income distribution.

Not only does economic consolidation exacerbate economic inequality among consumers, it also increases the economic disparities among workers. Top firms in concentrated sectors that enjoy abnormally high profits reward their employees with higher wages, a trend that is widening between-firm inequality.

Growing market power has also harmed the forces of economic dynamism. Consolidation helps explain, in part, the declining formation of new firms. The same barriers to competition that have allowed incumbent firms to expand their market share make it costlier for new firms to get off the ground. Declining startup activity means fewer incumbents face displacement by new competitors. This lack of competition contributes to private-sector underinvestment.

These trends deserve—and are beginning to receive—bipartisan attention. The Senate Subcommittee on Antitrust, Competition Policy and Consumer Rights convened a hearing on the subject. As testimony offered during the hearing made clear, the current debate features three different understandings of the purpose of antitrust legislation, and three different standards for judging when antitrust enforcement is warranted.

Three Theories of Antitrust

Both conservatives and progressives invoke "consumer welfare" as antitrust's core concern, but they offer divergent interpretations of this concept. Guided by the late Robert Bork's seminal work, *The Antitrust Paradox*, conservatives invoke a total welfare standard that regards efficiency-enhancing mergers as presumptively legitimate, no matter how those gains are allocated between consumers and producers. For their part, progressives also focus on the consequences for consumers, but employ a broader understanding of consumer welfare that encompasses quality, innovation, and choice as well as price.

A third stance entered the fray more recently. Populists regard the consumer welfare standard as inadequate because it pays no attention to the political dimension of antitrust—in particular, to the connection between economic concentration and corporate political power. Reflecting a tradition extending back a century to the thinking of Louis D. Brandeis, populists believe that a multiplicity of businesses is preferable to a small number of large firms—for the health of local communities as well as economic sectors—even if consumers pay higher prices.

Populists offer a plausible account of the historical record. From the beginning, antitrust legislation has reflected a wide range of concerns. Some advocates have objected to excessive economic concentration because of its effects on prices and competition. Others have emphasized the civic importance of preserving local businesses, protecting small producers against the superior market power of large corporations, and safeguarding political equality.

Nonetheless, the populist stance has left both conservatives and progressives worried that a radical revision of the current framework would mean transforming antitrust into an arena of political contention without clear standards to guide administrators and judges, ultimately weakening the antitrust regime.

The Best Way Forward

Despite our sympathy for the populists' historical understanding, we share these concerns. At the same time, we do not believe that the conservative interpretation of consumer welfare adequately reflects that animating purpose of antitrust legislation.

The need to both craft clear, predictable rules and renew vigorous enforcement inclines us toward the progressive approach, and it shapes the four proposals at the heart of our recent report.[1]

First, the antitrust agencies should reinvigorate the "structural presumption" against excessive sectoral concentration and tighten the enforcement standards for horizontal mergers. This includes lowering the threshold at which prospective mergers are subject to rigorous scrutiny. The current threshold at which antitrust scrutiny is triggered has failed to prevent harmful levels of concentration, as evidenced by the data outlined above. This permissive approach has directly contributed to rising concentration. The agencies should also rely on its "lookback" authority, reversing mergers if evidence emerges showing anticompetitive effects.

Second, the agencies should update the Non-Horizontal Merger Guidelines to reflect the reality that vertical integration can have anticompetitive effects. Revisions might include dismissing the presumption that nonhorizontal mergers are pro-competitive, paying special attention to acquisitions by dominant firms, and placing the burden of proof on the merging parties to demonstrate pro-consumer effects. Updated guidelines should acknowledge that remedies that make merger approval contingent on meeting behavioral criteria (such as Google's promise to the Federal Trade Commission not to pull content from user reviews from third-party sites) are often inadequate. Instead, as Makan Delrahim, assistant attorney general for the antitrust division of the U.S. Department of Justice, advocated in an address, the agencies should offer structural remedies, such as divestiture, as a substitute when needed.

Third, U.S. antitrust enforcement needs a new regime to deal with predatory pricing. There are few tools to wield against American antitrust. When episodes such as Mylan's 400% price hikes for its EpiPen product stoke public outrage, the government is forced to rely on hearings and public shaming to induce corporations to lower monopoly pricing, a strategy that often fails. A predatory pricing regime would also tackle price-cutting efforts that reduce but do not eliminate a dominant actor's profit margin but can force weaker actors to capitulate, rendering the market less competitive. For example, after Amazon's first attempt to acquire Quidsi was rejected, Amazon initiated a price war against Quidsi, a move that ultimately forced the competing e-commerce platform to merge with Amazon.

Fourth, the transaction costs of antitrust enforcement should be reduced. This would include reinstating a rule that has allowed automatic appeals of district courts' antitrust decisions to the Supreme Court, bypassing an entire level of appellate review. Expediting enforcement will alleviate the drain on agencies' resources that results from the current lengthy process. The longer that monopoly abuses are allowed to persist, the more entrenched offenders become, and the more unlawful rents they can extract from consumers. Forcing firms to disgorge these ill-gotten gains after the fact is difficult at best, and there is no way of compensating potential entrepreneurs that monopolistic firms deterred from starting new businesses.

These proposals, we conclude, will work best as the basis of a reformed 21st-century antitrust regime that can command bipartisan support.

TAKEAWAYS

Market consolidation is on the rise, bringing with it several negative economic consequences. It is exacerbating income inequality among consumers and increasing wage disparities among workers, further widening between-firm inequality.

✓ The framework that has guided antitrust enforcement for the last four decades is coming under intense scrutiny, but there are multiple schools of thought regarding the best path forward.

✓ Both conservatives and progressives invoke "consumer welfare" as antitrust's core concern, but they offer divergent interpretations of this concept. Populists regard the consumer welfare standard as inadequate because it pays no attention to the political dimension of antitrust.

✓ To reverse these troubling trends, antitrust agencies should:

   • Tighten the enforcement standards for horizontal mergers

- Reverse mergers if evidence shows anticompetitive effects

- Update their guidelines to reflect the reality that vertical integration can have anticompetitive effects

- Develop new tools to deal with predatory pricing

- Reduce the transaction costs of antitrust enforcement

NOTE

1. William A. Galston and Clara Hendrickson, "A Policy at Peace with Itself: Antitrust Remedies for Our Concentrated, Uncompetitive Economy," Brookings Institute, January 5, 2018, https://www.brookings.edu/research/a-policy-at-peace-with-itself-antitrust-remedies-for-our-concentrated-uncompetitive-economy/.

Adapted from content posted on hbr.org, January 9, 2019 (product #H043T0).

DON'T BREAK UP FACEBOOK—TREAT IT LIKE A UTILITY

by Dipayan Ghosh

Recently Facebook cofounder Chris Hughes joined a chorus of voices (including presidential hopeful Elizabeth Warren, Texas senator Ted Cruz, and former Secretary of Labor Robert Reich) arguing that regulatory agencies should apply antitrust authority to or even "break up" the digital giant.[1] Hughes positioned the move as a necessity to subvert the more insidious effects we have seen arise from Facebook and similar platforms, such as the spread of disinformation and hate speech.

His argument drew a great deal of popular support from the broad public as well as sharp criticism from the competition policy establishment. The company itself also pushed back, with newly minted public policy executive Nick Clegg penning a comeback arguing that breaking up Facebook would only serve to punish an innovative company that has created tremendous economic value.[2]

Critically, though, breaking up the company is not the only way to temper its destructive effects. I suggest an even more radical approach: I contend that Facebook and firms like it have become natural monopolies that necessitate a novel, stringent set of regulations to obstruct their capitalistic overreaches and protect the public against ingrained economic exploitation. While this option does not exclude the possibility of also pursuing a policy of breakup, I believe it is the more important objective and must take precedence. To understand why, we can apply rules of thumb from traditional competition and antitrust policy analysis, in which policy makers consider the economic dynamics of the industry in a stepwise manner.

The first step is to consider whether the industry in which the company operates is "competitive." To do so, the Justice Department's antitrust division and the Federal Trade Commission typically consider the relative market share of the firm in question. (Which agency actually makes the determination depends on the particular circumstance.) There is no explicit threshold for how much market share a company can have before it is considered a monopoly, though the FTC typically does not scrutinize a company for monopoly power if it occupies less than 50% of a market, while the lowest-ever market share determined to result in monopoly power by the European Commission was 39.7%. If the market appears competitive, you typically leave it alone; if it isn't (as, I would argue, is the case for the leading Silicon Valley digital giants), then you move to the next step of analysis.

Let's apply this to Facebook. The company's industry can be hard to define because the company's holdings and technological features change so quickly, as does the overall sector; the same can be said of the other large consumer internet firms. Given Facebook's many platforms—including Messenger, WhatsApp, Instagram, and the big blue app—the firm covers social media, photo sharing, and messaging, among other industries. Given this, I contend that, in the United States, Facebook has a dominating presence in each of its consumer areas of activity. This suggests that the primary markets in which it operates services are indeed no longer competitive.

Second, to move a competition policy inquiry forward in the United States, the company in question not only must be deemed to have excessive market share but must also be shown to use this market position to exploit the consumer—a standard that the judicial system has taken over time to mean consumer price hikes.

Many experts have contended that companies like Facebook and Google do not engage in such exploitation, because consumers are not charged money for access to even the highest revenue-generating services such as social media and search. But this conclusion is wrongheaded. Various forms of currency have lubricated various markets throughout history. The currency extracted from individuals in the consumer internet context is typically not money, but a novel, complex combination of the individual's personal data and attention. Given the market concentration exhibited by companies like Facebook and Google in their respective industry silos, one could suggest that these are pseudo-monopolistic firms that collect so much data and exploit so much of our attention in such invasive and questionable manners that they necessarily and systematically leave consumers in the lurch. As I discuss in a recent paper, these firms are two-sided platforms that have monopolized the consumer side; accordingly, they extract the end consumers' currency on one side of the platform at extortionate monopoly rates, and exchange it for monetary revenue at tremendously high margins on the other side of the platform.[3] It is this subtle but corrosive form of exploitation that policy makers should find most objectionable.

The third step is to examine the market to see whether fledgling entrepreneurs and other firms could someday compete in the industry. If so, then you should pursue a series of pro-competition policies. These may range from issuing targeted regulations that narrowly protect consumers from certain forms of harm to actively breaking them up. This is what Hughes and others have suggested for Facebook.

But if you cannot foresee any entrepreneur ever naturally competing with the incumbents, the prescription is entirely different. In this case, the firm is a "natural monopoly." Railroads, roadways, and telecommunications firms have in the past been considered natural monopolies because their costs of infrastructure and other barriers to entry suggest there should be no more than one player in each of those particular markets. When policy makers reach such a conclusion about a firm, they typically first attempt to institute a set of rigorous utility-like regulations so that consumers are protected from exploitation before considering other ancillary forms of regulatory policy. For example, the federal government regulates telecommunications firms' minimum levels of service for emergency calling and provides guidelines for their handling of consumer data.

I believe that the consumer internet is a kind of natural monopoly. Its leading constituent firms consistently exhibit network effects: The networked services operated by Facebook, Amazon, and Google increase in value when more users use them. This meanwhile makes it extraordinarily difficult for new entrants to offer competitive levels of utility to consumers out of the gate. As with telecommunications before it, this industry now maintains impossibly high barriers to entry. The leading internet companies have gradually established intricate, proprietary physical and digital infrastructures through the placement of new physical networks, the cultivation of preferential access to broadband providers and content owners, and the creation of an exclusive consumer tracking-and-targeting regime that necessarily shuts out the competition from access to the market for consumer data and attention. Furthermore, if a new entrepreneur does develop an innovative idea that picks up to a degree, an internet monopoly can readily acquire or copy it, and integrate it into its existing infrastructure. Given this, I believe there is no capacity for a second firm to effectively compete against Facebook in the market silos it dominates or the other internet giants in theirs.

Thus, while breaking up the firms may not be a bad idea, our first instinct should instead be to strike straight at the business model that makes these firms so dominant with clear and stringent regulations to protect the dynamism of markets and consumers themselves—not to mention the integrity of the media ecosystem and the openness of journalistic inquiry. Otherwise, companies like Facebook will likely continue to maintain and strengthen their monopoly positions, further building their hegemony over consumer data, industrial intelligence, and digital and physical infrastructure.

If we agree that firms like Facebook are natural monopolies, we should then begin to consider utility regulations that can effectively hold them accountable to the public. In the past, the United States has given such designations to both private and public monopolies (including, for instance, electric utilities) that have variously resulted in the creation of new regulatory agencies to treat monopolistic overreach. In the case of consumer internet firms, such regulations could entail stricter standards concerning user privacy and data processing; clear and consistent investigations of any proposed merger, acquisition, or growth of business into parallel industries, especially in cases where excess concentration or market bottlenecks could result; complete transparency into the ways that the industry's algorithms disseminate ads and content, particularly to marginalized classes of the population; taxes or stipulations to uplift public interests such as independent journalism and digital literacy; and minimum required investments in technologies that can detect and proactively act against obvious instances of hate speech and disinformation, among others.

All of this need not mean we should not also pursue breaking up these firms. But doing so may not effectively address the harms wrought by consumer internet firms with immediate effect and is thus a lesser imperative. What the U.S. government should in fact pursue are the overreaches of a business model that has systemically subverted the public interest and perpetuated a series of negative externalities in our media and information ecosystem. The economic design of the United States rightly gives the capitalistic market free sway to innovate—but when such commercialization breeds exploitation of the individual, our nation has always taken action to protect our democratic interests ahead of the freedom of markets. The consumer internet should be no different.

TAKEAWAYS

A chorus of voices is arguing that regulatory agencies should apply antitrust authority to, or even break up,

Facebook. But splitting up the company is not the only way to temper its most harmful effects.

- ✓ Facebook and other internet giants could be named natural monopolies. The United States has taken this approach in many other industries with high barriers to entry such as electric utilities, telecoms, and railroads.

- ✓ The natural monopoly designation would allow for the creation of new regulatory agencies to protect the public from economic exploitation by these companies.

- ✓ In the case of consumer internet firms, such regulations could entail stricter standards concerning user privacy and data processing; complete transparency into the ways that the industry's algorithms disseminate ads and content; and investments into technologies that can detect and proactively act against hate speech and disinformation.

NOTES

1. Chris Hughes, "It's Time to Break Up Facebook," *New York Times*, May 9, 2019, https://www.nytimes.com/2019/05/09/opinion/sunday/chris-hughes-facebook-zuckerberg.html.

2. Nick Clegg, "Breaking Up Facebook Is Not the Answer," *New York Times*, May 11, 2019, https://www.nytimes.com/2019/05/11/opinion/facebook-nick-clegg-chris-hughes.html.

3. Dipayan Ghosh, "A New Digital Social Contract to Encourage Internet Competition," *CPI Antitrust Chronicle*, April 2019.

Adapted from content posted on hbr.org, May 30, 2019 (product #H04YYW).

6

HOW MORE REGULATION FOR U.S. TECH COULD BACKFIRE

by Larry Downes

Over the past few years, tech companies have become lightning rods for everything from dissatisfaction over the 2016 U.S. presidential election to the possibility of a smartphone-driven dystopia.

Innovation and its discontents are nothing new, of course, going back at least to the 18th century, when Luddites physically attacked industrial looms. Hostility to the internet appeared the moment the web became a commercial technology, threatening from the outset to upend traditional businesses and maybe even our deeply embedded beliefs about family, society, and government. George Mason University's Adam Thierer, reviewing a resurgence of books about the "existential threat" of disruptive innovation, has detailed what he calls a "techno-panic template" in how we react to disruptive innovations that don't fit into familiar categories.[1]

But with the proliferation of new products and their reach ever deeper into our work, home, and personal lives, the relentless tech revolt shouldn't really come as any surprise, especially to those of us in Silicon Valley.

Still, the only solution critics can propose for our growing tech malaise is government intervention—usually expressed vaguely as "regulating tech" or "breaking up" the biggest and most successful internet companies. Breakups, which require a legal finding that the structure of a company is enabling anticompetitive behavior, seem now to have become a synonym for somehow crippling a successful enterprise.

Of course, nobody thinks technology companies should be left unregulated. Tech companies, like any other enterprise, are already subject to a complex tangle of laws, varying based on industry and local authority. They all pay taxes, report their finances, disclose significant shareholders, and comply with the full range of employment, health and safety, advertising, intellectual property, consumer protection, and anticompetition laws, to name just a few.

There are also specialized laws for tech, including limits on how internet companies can engage with children. In the United States, commercial drones must be registered with the Federal Aviation Administration. Genetic testing and other health-related devices must pass muster with the Food and Drug Administration. Increasingly, ride-sharing and casual rental services must meet some of the same standards and inspections as longtime transportation and hospitality incumbents.

There are growing calls, likewise, to regulate social media and video platforms as if they were traditional print or broadcast news sources, even though doing so would almost certainly run afoul of the very free speech protections proponents are hoping to preserve.

But perhaps what tech critics really want are more innovative rules. Traditional regulations, after all, were designed in response to earlier technologies and the market failures they generated. They don't cover largely speculative and mostly future-looking concerns.

What if, for example, artificial intelligence puts an entire generation out of work? What if genetic manipulations accidentally unravel the fabric of DNA, reversing evolution in one fell swoop? What if social media companies learn so much about us that they undermine—intentionally or otherwise—democratic institutions, creating a tyranny of unregulated big data controlled by a few unelected young CEOs?

The problem with such speculation is that it is just that. In deliberative government, legislators and regulatory agencies must weigh the often-substantial costs of proposed limits against their likely benefit, balanced against the harm of simply leaving in place the current legal status quo.

But there's no scientific method for estimating the risk of prematurely shutting down experiments that could yield important discoveries. There's no framework for preemptively regulating nascent industries and potential new technologies. By definition, they've caused no measurable harm.

In particular, breaking up the most successful internet and cloud-based companies only looks like a solution. It isn't. Antitrust is meant to punish dominant companies that use their leverage to raise costs for consumers. Yet the services provided by technology companies are often widely available at little or no cost. Many of the products and services of Amazon, Apple, Google, Facebook, and Microsoft—the internet giants referred to by the *New York Times* as "the frightful five"—are free for consumers.

More to the point, breakups almost always backfire. Think of the former AT&T, which was regulated as a monopoly utility until 1982, when the government changed its mind and split the company into component long-distance and regional phone companies. The sum of the parts actually increased in value—except for the long-distance company, which faded in the face of unregulated new competitors.

Then, over the next 20 years, the regional companies put themselves back together and, with economies of scale, reemerged as a mobile internet network and pay TV provider, competing with cable companies and fast-growing internet-based video services including YouTube, Amazon, and Netflix. What started as a regulatory punishment for AT&T led to an even bigger network of companies.

On the other hand, the constant threat of a forced divestiture can be disastrous for consumers and enterprise alike. IBM prevailed against multiple efforts to break it up along product lines but was so shaken by the decades-long experience that the company became dangerously timid about future innovations, missing the shifts first to client-server and then to internet-based computing architectures, nearly bankrupting the business.

Microsoft, similarly, was so distracted by its multiyear fight to avoid breakup by both U.S. and European regulators that it lost essential momentum. It mostly missed out on the mobile revolution and hesitated in responding to open-source alternatives to operating systems, desktop applications, and other software apps that seriously eroded the company's once-formidable competitive advantage.

These examples hint at an alternative to random and unproven new forms of regulation for emerging technologies: simply waiting for the next generation of innovations and the entrepreneurs who wield them to disrupt the supposed monopolists right out of their disagreeable behaviors, sometimes fatally.

It might seem that the companies in the frightful five have unbeatable leads in retailing and cloud services, social media, search, advertising, desktop operating systems, and mobile devices. But the landscape of business history is littered with the corpses of supposedly invulnerable giants. In our research on wildly successful enterprises that fail to find a second act, Paul Nunes and I note that the average life span of companies on the Standard & Poor's 500 has fallen from 67 years in the 1920s to just 15 years in 2018.

In the early years of the internet age, a half-dozen companies were serially crowned the victor in search, only to be unseated by more innovative technology soon after. Yahoo and others gave way to Google, just as BlackBerry faded in response to the iPhone. Myspace (remember it?) collapsed at the introduction of Facebook, which, at the time, was little more than a bit of software from a college student. Napster lost in court (no new laws were needed for that), leaving Apple to define a working market for digital music. And who remembers the alarm bells rung in 2000 when then-dominant ISP America Online merged with content behemoth Time Warner?

The best regulator of technology, it seems, is simply more technology. And despite fears that channels are blocked, markets are locked up, and gatekeepers have closed networks that the next generation of entrepreneurs need to reach their audience, somehow they do it anyway—often embarrassingly fast, whether the presumed tyrant being deposed is a longtime incumbent or last year's startup darling.

That, in any case, is the theory on which U.S. policy makers across the political spectrum have nurtured technology-based innovation since the founding of the republic. Taking the long view, it's clearly been a winning strategy, especially when compared with the more invasive, command-and-control approach taken by the European Union, which continues to lag on every measure of the internet economy. (Europe's strategy now seems to be little more than to hobble U.S. tech companies and hope for the best.) Or compared with China, which has built tech giants of its own, but only by limiting outside access to its singularly enormous local market. And always with the risk that too much success by Chinese entrepreneurs may one day crash headfirst into a political culture that is deeply uncomfortable with the internet's openness.

That solution—to stay the course, to continue leaving tech largely to its own correctives—is cold comfort to those who believe tomorrow's problems, coming up fast in the rearview mirror, are both unprecedented and catastrophic.

Yet, so far there's no evidence supporting shrill predictions of a technology-driven apocalypse. Or that existing safeguards—both market and legal—won't save us from our worst selves.

Nor has tech's growing list of critics proposed anything more specific than simply calling for "regulation" to save us. Perhaps that's because effective remedies are incredibly hard to design.

The now-common calls to "regulate" and "break up" big tech companies may seem novel. But given the history of backlash against new technologies in general, and internet-based technologies in particular, the recent revolt against big tech companies comes as no surprise.

✓ Effective regulatory remedies are incredibly hard to design, and tech's growing list of critics haven't proposed measures that will be up to the challenge.

✓ What tech critics really want are more innovative rules. Traditional regulations were designed in response to earlier technologies and the market failures they generated. They don't cover largely speculative and mostly future-looking concerns. There's no framework for preemptively regulating nascent industries and potential new technologies.

✓ Though it might seem that the tech giants have unbeatable leads in retailing and cloud services, social media, search, advertising, desktop operating systems, and mobile devices, the landscape of business history is littered with the corpses of invulnerable giants.

NOTE

1. Adam Thierer, "Franklin Foer's Tech-Panic Manifesto," *Reason*, January 2018, http://reason.com/archives/2017/12/23/how-to-write-a-tech-panic-mani/.

Adapted from content posted on hbr.org, February 9, 2018 (reprint #H045VE).

Section 3

COMPETING AGAINST GIANTS

7

THE AMAZON-WHOLE FOODS DEAL MADE EVERY OTHER RETAILER'S PLAN OBSOLETE

by Darrell K. Rigby

When Amazon announced it would acquire Whole Foods Market, Amazon's stock price rose 2.4% on the news, increasing its market capitalization by $11 billion. At the same time, the price of SuperValu plummeted 14.4%, Kroger dropped 9.2%, and Sprouts fell 6.3%. You could almost hear the three-year plans of every grocer, and nearly every other traditional retailer, grinding through the shredding machines.

Nobody in the industry should be surprised that the future of retailing is moving toward a fusion of digital and physical experiences. However, Amazon's announcement made the nature and speed of that movement far more challenging. Too many traditional retailers have built their plans on three questionable premises: (1) they can add digital capabilities faster than Amazon can add stores; (2) Amazon's competitive space (e-commerce) is still constrained to a small percentage of U.S. retail sales; and (3) store-based retailers could profitably transition to a digital world by growing e-commerce sales cautiously enough to avoid diluting earnings and cannibalizing higher-margin store sales, while retreating to the most profitable stores and product categories that would be hardest for Amazon to attack. Until Amazon's announcement, food was considered such a safe haven.

Now it's clear that Amazon aims to sell customers everything, and therefore no retail spaces are safe. If Amazon can acquire its way into groceries, what will prevent it from entering department stores—as Alibaba has done in China—or furniture and appliance stores, electronics stores, or even drugstores? Moreover, if Amazon decides to use groceries to increase the frequency of customer deliveries, imagine the range of products it could quickly and profitably pile onto home delivery vehicles (or perhaps even provide for customer pickup). From now on, the only viable retail strategy is to try to advance and merge digital and physical capabilities faster and better than Amazon does. That means retailers must learn to compete head-on with Amazon in two fundamental capabilities: agile innovation and expense management.

Amazon's greatest competitive advantage is not its e-commerce network; it is its innovation engine. To understand this strength, take a look at the sample of innovations in figure 7-1. The successes were impressive even before 2007, when Amazon was smaller than Bed Bath & Beyond, J.C. Penney, or SuperValu are today. Back in 2005, Amazon Prime was conceived, developed, and launched in about two months. Note also the innovation efforts that Amazon has abandoned (highlighted in bold in the figure and making up about 25% of this sample). Many retailers would consider these failures, but most of them contributed valuable learning toward eventual hits. For example, Amazon abandoned Auctions and zShops, yet both laid the groundwork for the enormous success of Amazon Marketplace.

To compete with Amazon's relentless flow of innovations, traditional retailers have no choice but to relearn how to innovate like the successful startups they once

FIGURE 7-1

A sampling of Amazon's innovations over time

The company has abandoned about a quarter of them.

> Active innovation
> **Abandoned (Year)**

Year	Innovation
1995	Customer reviews
1997	1-Click ordering
	Recommendations
1999	Wish lists
	Electronics store
	Amazon Auctions (2000)
	zShops (2007)
2001	"Where's My Stuff?"
2002	Free shipping
2003	Marketplace
2004	**A9 search portal (2008)**
2005	Amazon Prime
	Private labels
2006	Elastic Compute Cloud web service
	Fulfillment by Amazon
	Askville (2013)
	Unbox (2015)
2007	Subscribe & Save
	Amazon Kindle
	Amazon Music
	AmazonFresh
	Endless.com (2012)
	Amazon WebPay (2014)
2009	Local express delivery (same day)
	PayPhrase (2012)
2010	Price Check
	Amazon Studios
	Webstore (2016)
2011	Appstore for Android
	Kindle Owners' Lending Library
	Amazon Lockers
	MyHabit (2016)
	Amazon Local (2015)
	Test Drive (2015)

Year	Innovation
2012	Amazon Media Group
	Music Importer (2015)
	AmazonSupply (later Amazon Business)
2013	Exclusive Prime Instant Videos
	Sunday delivery
	Anticipatory shipping
	Kindle Mayday
	AmazonSmile
2014	"Flow" image recognition in mobile app
	Amazon Prime Now (1-2 hours)
	Prime Pantry
	Fire TV
	Fire Phone (2015)
	Amazon Elements diapers (2015)
	Prime Photos
	Prime Music
	Amazon Local Register (2015)
	Amazon Wallet (2015)
2015	Amazon Echo
	Dash Buttons
	Amazon Launchpad
	Amazon Bookstore
	Amazon Destinations (2015)
	Amazon Restaurants
	Handmade at Amazon
	Amazon Home Services
2016	Prime Air
	Amazon Go
	Wickedly Prime
	Apparel private label
2017	Amazon STEM Club
	Amazon Chime
	Echo Look
	Echo Chime

Source: Bain & Co. analysis of Amazon.com

were. This innovation in innovation requires moving from predictive plans (based on increasingly unpredictable market conditions) to adaptive, agile innovation teams. Agile innovation teams are small. Amazon CEO Jeff Bezos famously believes that if you can't feed a team with two pizzas, it is too large. They're also multidisciplinary (with all the digital and physical skills to complete the task), are self-governing, and are geared for rapid pivots rather than predictable straightaways. These teams value creative working environments more than hierarchical bureaucracies, working prototypes over excessive documentation, customer collaboration over fixed specifications, and response to change over adherence to plans.

Yet many traditional retailers still lack the digital expertise and the right focus to make their teams succeed. Three out of four consumers say that they want more technology in stores and are more likely to visit stores that use technology effectively. But one major cross-industry study found that 70% of consumers feel that companies are getting the digital experience wrong. Indeed, many retailers are guilty of offering splashy virtual reality rooms, digital displays, and voice commands that consumers say don't work as expected, are not convenient, are hard to use, and are confusing. While executives aim to give consumers an increased sense of control and appeal to the most digitally savvy, consumers say they want technology that simply saves them time, increases convenience, and gets faster results.

A few smaller retailers, including Warby Parker and Rebecca Minkoff, are frequently cited for getting the digital-physical fusion right. Some major players have invested to raise their game. Walmart, for example, made digitally focused acquisitions including Jet.com (with its Smart Cart algorithms), Bonobos, and Moosejaw to acquire technology, talent, and customers. It has developed next-gen stores, installed pickup towers and an automated online grocery pickup facility, rolled out Walmart Pay and Scan & Go technologies allowing customers to avoid checkout lines, and touted free two-day shipping for online orders, even testing associate deliveries of those orders. Most important, it is changing the culture, increasing the pace of innovation, obsessing over customer experience, and improving results.

But there are two major challenges for traditional retailers hoping to accelerate their innovation engines: First, it's expensive; second, many retailers have delayed innovation funding for so long that the "strategic debt" seems overwhelming.

To give you a sense of the expense required, Amazon reported in one recent year that it spent over $16 billion (11.8% of sales) on "technology and content." This is not all innovation R&D or IT, but it's mostly that. Meanwhile, Gartner reports that retail and wholesale companies spend about 1.5% of sales on IT. (Most of my retail clients seem to fall into the 2%–3% range.) Research and advisory firm IHL Group asked top retail CIOs how much their IT budgets are currently increasing and how much they should increase to compete against Amazon. The answer: Budgets are growing by 4.7% but would need to increase 87% to 237% to start closing the gap.[1]

How will retailers find this kind of money? By reallocating spending away from people and activities that matter more to managers than to customers. An effective approach applies the same kinds of agile innovation teams that develop new products to the improvement of processes and business models. Retailers love to say that "retail is detail," but perfecting increasingly irrelevant business models is wasting money that is desperately needed to fund innovative growth. Substantial amounts of money often lie fallow in the debilitating layers of approval required for innovations or other urgent decisions, in the artificial accuracy of trying to make perfect predictions, and in manual processes that could be done better, faster, and cheaper with machine learning.

The retail world has learned the limitations of predictive planning compared with adaptive innovation in an increasingly unpredictable market. Going forward, retailers will need to rapidly and radically adapt their lists of strategic initiatives, the prioritization and sequencing of those initiatives, as well as the speed and funding of their execution. We'll know traditional retailers are getting it right when announcements of breakthrough innovations start driving up their stock prices, finally raising doubts about Amazon's ability to respond.

TAKEAWAYS

Amazon's acquisition of Whole Foods Market showed that tech giants can enter and reshape nearly any industry without warning. How can retailers compete?

✓ Retailers must try to advance and merge digital and physical capabilities faster and better than Amazon and best the powerhouse in two fundamental capabilities: agile innovation and expense management.

✓ To compete with Amazon's relentless flow of innovations, traditional retailers need to relearn how to innovate like the successful startups they once were, moving from predictive plans to adaptive, agile innovation teams.

✓ Retailers will need to invest radically more in R&D to compete head-on with the tech giants. To free up the resources necessary, they will need to reallocate spending away from activities that don't matter to customers.

NOTE

1. Greg Buzek, "Amazon Has a TIGIR by the Tail," IHL Group Analyst Corner, January 25, 2017, https://www.ihlservices.com /news/analyst-corner/2017/01/amazon-has-a-tigir-by-the-tail/.

Adapted from "The Amazon–Whole Foods Deal Means Every Other Retailer's Three-Year Plan Is Obsolete," on hbr.org, June 21, 2017 (product #H03QOS).

8

WHAT BIG CONSUMER BRANDS CAN DO TO COMPETE IN A DIGITAL ECONOMY

by Howard Yu

No industry is failing faster than retail. The 125-year-old Sears—once the world's largest retailer—filed for bankruptcy. The public has more or less come to expect the shuttering of stores such as Macy's, Sears, Toys "R" Us, Kmart, Kohl's, J.C. Penney, and Barnes & Noble. The ones that manage to escape are discount chains—such as T.J. Maxx and Marshalls—which compete aggressively on price.

Price competition hurts. It also hurts the brands sold inside the stores, which in part explains why consumer product giants like Procter & Gamble are seeing their sales stagnate for products like Tide detergent, Gillette razors, Pampers diapers, and Crest toothpaste.

A report by the consultancy BCG documented a general decline in sales among consumer packaged goods (CPG) companies in the United States during 2017, with midsized and large companies losing market share and small companies increasing theirs.[1] Consultancy Catalina also revealed that 90 of the 100 top brands had all lost market share. In dollar terms, small players—defined as those with sales of less than $1 billion—grabbed approximately $15 billion in sales from their larger peers between 2012 and 2017.

Shoppers now purchase more online, making fewer trips to stores and seeing fewer in-store promotions. A small but trendy razor club with a hip logo, Harry's, attracts more Instagram followers and product subscriptions through its website than a fully stocked Gillette aisle in a supermarket ever could. And so Harry's grew 35% year-on-year over a three-year period, three times faster than the industry average, commanding 9% of all online razor sales.

Whereas the Gillette aisle in the local supermarket targets exactly one neighborhood, Harry's website reaches millions. Harry's bolsters the subscription habits of its recurring consumers, whereas Gillette relies on in-store impulse buying. When someone buys a razor in a store, Gillette has no clue who's buying what and when; Harry's knows it all.

Newcomers like Harry's still represent only a fraction of the overall market, but they've captured the majority of the growth in that time—a defining feature of disruptive innovation. That's why P&G has been restructuring for 20 years "without much to show for it," according to one former finance manager. No matter how well P&G reorganizes itself, it can't reverse the decline from $83 billion in sales in 2008 to $65 billion in 2017 without learning some new tricks.

The *Wall Street Journal* reported that the sluggish sales of Johnson & Johnson baby shampoo have forced the company to make a desperate bet.[2] J&J will take out the yellow dye from its iconic golden-hued baby shampoo and make it clear. Whether this will help J&J in the long run, no one knows. But the sluggish sales reflect the same dynamics that P&G has been facing: market share lost to smaller brands, overreliance on traditional retailers, and an inability to create direct relationships with consumers at a time when e-commerce is exploding.

P&G went to war to clean up the online ad market and used its pull as the world's biggest advertiser to squeeze out more information about the effectiveness of digital ads for Google and Facebook. It slashed digital ad expenditures by more than $200 million and issued an ultimatum for tech firms to become more transparent. That's a good start. But it also needs a new vision.

Activist investor Nelson Peltz, who sits on P&G's board, has such a vision. He argued that P&G "must acknowledge that others will inevitably come up with new ideas, new opportunities for growth, and new products that are on-trend with consumers." He also suggested that "P&G must be proficient at acquiring small, midsize, and local brands and using its R&D and marketing clout to take them to the next level."[3]

What Peltz suggested is exactly what Xiaomi is already doing.

Xiaomi's Startup Incubator

By March 2016, Chinese smartphone maker Xiaomi had invested in some 55 startups, generating products from power banks to air purifiers. Of these companies, 29 were incubated from the ground up by Xiaomi, and four were already unicorns worth over $1 billion. What

Xiaomi offers to startups is a combination of funding and incubation by "taking non-controlling shares" and "leaving maximum interests to the startups" so that "they are much more incentivized and willing to fight on the front line," explained Liu De, cofounder and vice president of Xiaomi.[4]

Startups typically get access to Xiaomi's brand and distribution—its online channel, its app, and its 300 offline stores. As a result, Xiaomi is poised as not only a low-cost phone maker but also an emerging powerhouse among the makers of the all-important "connected home devices." "Our ecosystem even gives customers unusual new products that they never knew existed," said Wang Xiang, Xiaomi's senior vice president, referring to the company's Bluetooth speaker, internet-enabled rice cooker, and air purifier (the first affordable one in China)—products that the company claims are not only best in class but also cost less than their existing counterparts.[5]

P&G should follow suit. It can no longer be a mere "industrial corporation with a future based on technology" but rather must become a house of startup brands that runs pop-up stores, makes home deliveries, celebrates communities with parties, fosters subscription models, and curates compelling product personas, all while gathering comprehensive consumer data to guide new product innovation. In effect, it becomes a sort of coherent conglomerate. It makes a lot of bets, owns numerous largely separate businesses, but uses a few key central-ized capabilities like branding and retail distribution to provide each of its subsidiaries with something indepen-dent CPG companies can't match.

This structure would better enable P&G to copy what scrappy upstarts like Harry's or Warby Parker do. These startups, despite being manufacturers, digitalize all cus-tomer touchpoints (like Netflix), control the user expe-rience by forward-integrating into the brick-and-mortar realm (like Amazon buying Whole Foods), and then run data analytics to optimize merchandise mix and inform product innovation (like Alibaba's Taobao).

So, are such steps too bold for a CPG giant from Cin-cinnati? The 180-year-old house of brands hasn't managed to survive this long without making bold steps in the past.

When the first boxes of Tide went on sale in 1946, it was the first synthetic detergent that could deep-clean clothing "without making colors dull or dingy." Before Tide, all soaps were "naturally" made by heating animal or vegetable fats with water and an alkali base. The bene-fits of a synthetic detergent that made "white clothes look whiter" were so apparent that within just three years, Tide outstripped all other brands on the market and be-came the number-one detergent. In the wake of Tide's introduction, P&G would "no longer be a soap company" but "would become an industrial corporation with its future based on technology," its technical staff body tripling that of the pre-Tide year of 1945.

But inside P&G, managers had feared the new products might cannibalize their beloved Ivory soap. Only Chairman William Cooper Procter, the last family manager of P&G, remained a staunch supporter of synthetic detergents. In a memorable remark addressed to his staff, he said, "[T]his [synthetic detergent] may ruin the soap business. But if anybody is going to ruin the soap business, it had better be Procter & Gamble."

P&G made bold moves to save itself in the past. Now it just needs to rediscover that chairman's mentality. And that might well go for any consumer brand, not least P&G, looking to escape the utter ruins of the retail wasteland.

TAKEAWAYS

Large consumer packaged goods (CPG) companies like P&G are losing market share to new entrants. They are challenged by an overreliance on traditional retailers and an inability to create direct relationships with consumers at a time when e-commerce is exploding.

✓ To grow outside traditional retail, CPG companies can learn from their new competitors by running pop-up stores, making home deliveries, celebrating communities, fostering subscription models, and curating compelling product personas, all while gathering comprehensive consumer data to guide new product innovation.

✓ CPG companies should become a sort of coherent conglomerate. They must make a lot of bets, own numerous, largely separate businesses, but use a few key centralized capabilities like branding and retail distribution to provide each of their subsidiaries with something their competitors can't match.

✓ CPG companies can learn from Xiaomi, the Chinese smartphone maker that placed bets by investing in some 55 startups. The result? Twenty-nine took off and four are already unicorns worth over $1 billion.

NOTES

1. Peri Edelstein et al., "What the Fastest-Growing CPG Companies Do Differently," BCG, June 14, 2018, https://www.bcg.com/en-us/publications/2018/what-fastest-growing-consumer-packaged-goods-companies-do-differently.aspx.

2. Jonathan D. Rockoff, "Bringing Up Baby's Market Share at J&J," *Wall Street Journal*, October 27, 2018, https://www.wsj.com/articles/bringing-up-babys-market-share-at-j-j-1540612886.

3. Trian Partners, "Revitalize P&G Together," white paper, September 6, 2017, https://trianpartners.com/content/uploads/2017/01/Trian-PG-White-Paper-9.6.17-1.pdf.

4. Rita Liao, "Inside Xiaomi: The Perks and Perils of Startups That Join Its Ecosystem," *Tech in Asia*, March 26, 2018, https://www.techinasia.com/xiaomi-ecosystem.

5. Shoshanna Delventhal, "How Xiaomi Makes Money," Investopedia, July 30, 2019, https://www.investopedia.com/news/how-xiaomi-makes-money/#ixzz5F8e000tB.

Adapted from content posted on hbr.org, December 4, 2018 (product #H04OF9).

9

CRAFTING A STRATEGY IN THE AGE OF GIANTS

lassic strategic concepts like the five forces, blue oceans, and core competencies are familiar, brilliant, and useful, but they aren't the final word in competition. The rules of strategy have never been static and the ascent of the tech giants is reshaping them once again. As always, no approach is one-size-fits-all. For some companies, the answer will be to become bigger, broader, faster, and more like the tech monopolies. Others will need to remain focused deliberately, honing a few unmatchable capabilities, brands, or services. The four short pieces that follow will help you rethink your company's strategy to compete and win among the giants.

THE OLD AND NEW RULES OF COMPETITIVE ADVANTAGE

by Julian Birkinshaw

Warren Buffett is famous for investing in businesses that have what strategists call "deep moats." The moat is what protects the business from competitors. Sometimes it is based on access to a scarce resource or ownership of a patent, sometimes it is based on customer loyalty and a strong brand, and sometimes it is an artifact of government regulation.

How do you build a moat? One approach is to position your business skillfully, by finding an industry with high entry barriers and then differentiating your product to keep customers hooked in. The other approach is to focus on your underlying assets and capabilities, to invest in those assets that are rare, valuable, and hard for competitors to imitate.

These two worldviews—market positioning and the resource-based view—have dominated how we have thought about competitive advantage for 40 years.

But the rapid growth of business ecosystems in recent years challenges this thinking. Most of these ecosystem orchestrators, like Google, Alibaba, and Uber, don't make the things they sell; they exist to link others together, and this makes the old positioning-based logic less relevant. And, of course, they don't have many assets, either. They create value through relationships and networks, not through physical goods or infrastructure, so arguments built around asset ownership are equally challenging. These firms are also looking to grow the market—by increasing the flow of people and goods—rather than to capture as much of the existing market as possible.

In other words, they don't care much for the moat-based logic of competitive advantage. I think a more apt metaphor for these firms may be the logic of the turnstile: They want to get as many players involved in their ecosystem as possible, and to get them interacting according to rules they have shaped. Of course, there are many ways these companies make money—committees, membership fees, advertising sales, and so on—but the key point with all these business models is that they work better when the ecosystem is larger. That's why the turnstile metaphor is useful.

This shift from moats to turnstiles can be hard to grasp. For most business strategists, it is second nature to protect your existing assets and to keep competition at bay. But a pure-play orchestrator is happy to open up to competition and to share its intellectual property, as long as that keeps the ecosystem growing. Its aim is to maximize the number of people coming through the turnstile, rather than to increase the height of the fence or the width of the moat.

NETFLIX'S ANSWER TO COMPETING WITH AMAZON

by Walter Frick

Amazon doesn't just want to be the place where you do your online shopping. It wants to be where you watch TV, how you interact with your home, the infrastructure behind your favorite websites—even the place where you do whatever offline shopping is left after its e-commerce behemoth is done gobbling up brick-and-mortar retail.

But is the only strategy in our winner-take-all era to get as big as possible, to aspire to eventually serve everyone, and to meet their every need?

Netflix's Reed Hastings doesn't think so. Of course, Netflix is no mom-and-pop operation. But in a telling interview with Recode, Hastings explicitly rejected the Bezos approach of strategy-as-world-domination. When asked why Netflix has no plans to add live sports, he explained:

> We're not trying to meet all needs. So, Amazon's business strategy is super broad. Meet all needs. I mean, the stuff that will be in Prime in 5 or 10 years will be amazing, right? And so we can't try to be that—we'll never be as good as them at what they're trying to be. What we can be is the emotional connection brand, like HBO or Netflix. So, think of it as they're trying to be Walmart, we're trying to be Starbucks. So, super focused on one thing that people are very passionate about.[1]

Michael Porter would approve. "The essence of strategy is choosing what *not* to do," he writes in his 1996 classic "What Is Strategy?" In Porter's view, sustainable competitive advantage depends on trade-offs, including the fact that it's difficult for one company to serve all customers across a wide range of needs. "A company known for delivering one kind of value may lack credibility and confuse customers—or even undermine its reputation—if it delivers another kind of value or attempts to deliver two inconsistent things at the same time," Porter writes.

Hastings is betting that Porter's rules haven't been repealed. Do strategic trade-offs really limit Amazon's ability to compete with Netflix? It's hard to say. Maybe digital technology and the changing economies of scale really have changed the nature of competition. But for most companies, trying to compete on scale with tech's frightful five is a losing gambit. And if you were to bet on which firms would manage to thrive alongside the giants, you could do worse than picking ones like Netflix, where the CEO is thinking hard about trade-offs and differentiation.

In an era where a small number of huge companies have unprecedented reach and control, Porter's central question seems more important than ever: What *won't* you be?

WALMART WON'T STAY ON TOP IF ITS STRATEGY IS "COPY AMAZON"

by Denise Lee Yohn

Walmart has made a series of moves to fight Amazon and grow its e-commerce business. It purchased Jet.com and installed Jet's founder, Marc Lore, as head of its e-commerce division. It has also been acquiring e-commerce niche players, including Shoebuy and outdoor gear retailer Moosejaw, and digital technology companies, such as search experts Adchemy and cloud platform OneOps.

Walmart does need to shore up its e-commerce capabilities, but its attempts to out-Amazon Amazon aren't a winning strategy. For one thing, by offering the new shipping service, Walmart is really only playing catch-up. Lore himself described free shipping as table stakes. And Amazon is adding new benefits to Prime membership continuously.

Walmart can't compete with Amazon Prime's value proposition, at least not yet. Walmart's acquisitions of e-commerce companies and digital technologies, and the talent that comes along with them, enable it to get better at this, but Amazon will continue to improve too.

Trying to beat Amazon at its own game is not only likely to fail, it's also not in Walmart's best interests. Walmart has perhaps the best physical distribution and retail network *in the world*. It needs to be competitive on digital channels, sure. But, more important, it should excel at brick-and-mortar. Improving the in-store experience, promoting omnichannel shopping and fulfillment options, and developing in-person service innovations are avenues that leverage its brand equity and core competencies— and they're approaches that would put Amazon at a disadvantage. Walmart should invest to advance its strongest competitive advantage: its physical stores.

The company's obsession with competing with Amazon also seems to have taken Walmart's focus off its brand identity in everyday low prices. In its announcements and ads about the new free shipping service, product prices have not been mentioned. Walmart has held a low-price leadership position from its start. Now, in some cases, it can often offer *lower* prices than Amazon because Jet.com's operating model doesn't rely on holding inventory. But the company has not initially elected to make its new pricing capabilities or its long-standing low prices part of its marketing efforts for e-commerce.

Many companies feel a pull to imitate the practices of successful rivals. But this rarely ends well. Core competencies stagnate, customers become confused, and the opportunity to lead instead of follow is squandered.

IN THE ECOSYSTEM ECONOMY, WHAT'S YOUR STRATEGY?

by Michael G. Jacobides

Many firms assume they should be the focus and chief architect of any ecosystem they create. That's not necessarily the case; sometimes you are better off sharing the role or being a complementor.

If you lack the qualifications to build an ecosystem but have an IP-protected product or service that could anchor one, your best bet most likely involves attracting the interest of a large company that could buy into or license your idea. If a small-scale HVAC installer had come up with a remotely controllable thermostat, it probably could not have attracted the ecosystem of complementors that

Google did. But it could have approached Google with the idea and served as a complementor while benefiting from licensing revenue. For many medium-size firms, a key strategy is to embed in many ecosystems. LIFX, for instance, connects with customers through Amazon's Alexa, Google Home, and Apple HomeKit.

Even if you bring a great product or service to the party and have the organizational and cultural capabilities to attract complementors, it might make sense to orchestrate in partnership with another firm in order to reach critical mass. Daimler and BMW recently announced plans to jointly create a managed-mobility ecosystem combining car sharing, ride hailing, parking, and other services. Concerned about disruption from firms such as Uber and Lyft, the automakers decided to collaborate on high-end services anchored to their brands—their chief differentiator and element of value, which a wholesale migration to mobility-as-a-service (MaaS) might well erode.

A big company can also buy into an ecosystem, which can be particularly helpful if its contribution is interchangeable with other firms' offerings. Toyota recently invested $1.5 billion in the Southeast Asian ride-hailing company Grab, reasoning that MaaS will drive demand for reliable low-cost cars. That partnership, the company hopes, will give Toyota not just a direct edge as a car supplier but also an understanding of car usage patterns that could confer an advantage over rivals such as Hyundai and Nissan.

While the hub economy may be upending some of the last century's rules of strategy—and even the last decade's—it remains as important as ever for companies to understand their unique strategic advantages and opportunities.

✓ The "build a moat" logic of competitive advantage often no longer applies when you are working with large business ecosystems and platforms. A "turn-stile" metaphor for allowing more companies to coexist in an ecosystem is more appropriate.

✓ Aspiring to be a giant is not a winning strategy for most companies. To thrive among the giants, smaller companies should think hard about trade-offs, differentiation, and deciding what they *won't* be.

✓ Simply imitating the practices of successful rivals can result in the stagnation of core competencies and cause customer confusion. Instead, companies should continue to invest in their unique competitive advantages.

✓ Companies may assume that they need to be the chief architect of any ecosystem in which they participate—but often they're better off sharing the role, being a complementor, or buying into a jointly owned ecosystem.

NOTE

1. Kurt Wagner, "Netflix CEO Reed Hastings: The Full Code Interview Video," Vox, June 4, 2017, https://www.vox.com/2017 /6/4/15730694/watch-netflix-ceo-reed-hastings-binge-watching -movies-tv-sports-code-interview-video.

Adapted from "Ecosystem Businesses Are Changing the Rules of Strategy," on hbr.org, August 8, 2019 (product #H053C3); "How Can Companies Compete with Amazon? Netflix Has the Answer," on hbr.org, June 19, 2017 (product #H03QOI); "Walmart Won't Stay on Top If Its Strategy Is 'Copy Amazon'," on hbr.org, March 21, 2017 (product #H03JHR); and "In the Ecosystem Economy, What's Your Strategy?" in Harvard Business Review, *September–October 2019 (product #R1905J).*

WHO WILL WIN THE INDUSTRIAL INTERNET?

by Vijay Govindarajan

J ust the announcement that Jeff Bezos, Warren Buffett, and Jamie Dimon will be entering the healthcare space sent shock waves to industry incumbents such as CVS, Cigna, and UnitedHealth. It also put a fundamental question back on the agendas of CEOs in other industries: Will software eat the world, as Marc Andreessen famously quipped? Is this a warning shot that signals that other legacy industrial companies, such as

Ford, Deere, and Rolls-Royce, are also at increased risk of being disrupted?

To start to answer that question, let's tally up the score. There are three types of products today. Digital natives (Amazon, Google, Facebook, Microsoft, IBM) have gained competitive advantage in the first two, and the jury is still out on the third:

- **Type 1:** These are "pure" information goods, where digital natives rule. An example would be Google in search, or Facebook in social networking. Their business models benefit from internet connectivity, and they enjoy tremendous network effects.

- **Type 2:** These are once-analog products that have now been converted into digital products, such as photography, books, and music. Here too, digital natives dominate. These products are typically sold as a service via digital distribution platforms (Audible.com for books, Spotify for music, Netflix for movies).

- **Type 3:** Then there are products where the input-output efficiency and reliability of the physical components are still critical, but digital is becoming an integral part of the product itself (in effect, computers are being put inside products). This is the world of the internet of things (IoT) and the industrial internet.

Manufacturing-heavy companies such as Caterpillar, Ford, and Rolls-Royce compete in this world. An aircraft engine is unlikely to become a purely digital product any time soon. Such products have three components: physical, "smart" (sensors, controls, microprocessors, software, and enhanced user interface), and connectivity (one machine connected to another machine; one machine connected to many machines; and many machines connected to each other in a system).

Digital natives have already disrupted industries such as media, publishing, travel, music, and photography. But who is likely to assume leadership in creating and capturing economic value in Type 3 products: Digital natives or industry incumbents? Ford or Tesla? Rolls-Royce or IBM? Caterpillar or Microsoft? A combination of Amazon, Berkshire Hathaway, and JPMorgan Chase or UnitedHealth?

The Challenges for Digital Natives

Value will no doubt be created in the era of smart, connected machines. We don't expect Amazon or Microsoft or IBM to design, make, and market agricultural tractors, aircraft engines, or MR scanners. The question really is: Can digital natives develop software-enabled solutions that siphon off significant value from industrial hardware? The answer is yes. But it won't be easy. It will require tremendous amounts of investments in building new capabilities for hardware companies like HP, Cisco, Dell, Samsung, and Lenovo; established software companies like Facebook, Google, Amazon, and Microsoft; and startups. In particular, there are three barriers they must overcome:

1. The physics of the hardware

Companies like Rolls-Royce design and manufacture jet engines. These are very complicated machines. There is hard science behind these machines. That's much different from digital natives like Airbnb where marketing is more important than technical expertise.

Industry incumbents have expertise in the material sciences, for instance. Further, scientific knowledge keeps improving over time. They have made heavy R&D investments—both basic and applied—to remain at the cutting edge of the physics of the hardware. Much of this scientific knowledge is protected by patents.

Mastery of hard science is a prerequisite to develop software-based solutions on the hardware. These companies' superior product/domain knowledge provides them the comparative advantage to model the asset's performance and write high-end/high-value-added software applications. A pure digital company can write commodity software applications. But it must acquire enough capabilities on the physics to write sophisticated apps that improve assets' performance.

2. Customer intimacy

Industrial giants have well-established brands, have built strong customer relationships, and have signed long-term service contracts. They've won customers' trust, which is why customers are willing to share data. Digital natives can work with industrial customers, but they have to first earn their trust; they must build capabilities to understand customer operations; they must match the industrials' cumulative learning from customer interactions; they must learn to ask for the right data; and they have to hire experts in several verticals that can turn data into insights.

3. Difficulty in sharing risks

Industrial incumbents have product knowledge, customer relationships, and field engineers on customer sites. Companies like Rolls-Royce can, therefore, offer outcome deals where they guarantee customer outcomes (for example, zero downtime, higher speed, more fuel efficiency, zero operator error, greater reliability) and share risks and rewards with customers. It would be very hard for Amazon or Google to guarantee customer outcomes and take risks with businesses whose operations they know little about.

The Challenges for Industrial Giants

Can the industrial giants lead in the industrial internet? The answer is yes. But it won't be easy for them, either. They too have three significant barriers to overcome.

1. Software talent

The IT talent in industrial companies can execute projects oriented toward process efficiency and cost reduction. That talent is ill-suited to develop new, breakthrough software products that offer superior customer outcomes. To that end, they must be able to attract world-class innovators and software engineers. Do young tech employees consider, say, Rolls-Royce, the same way as Facebook and Google? Not really. If so, how can the industrial giants compete to attract the best talent?

2. Digital culture

Industrial businesses and digital businesses operate with completely different principles. The characteristics of hardware businesses include a long product development cycle, Six Sigma efficiency, and a long sales cycle. Software businesses have different characteristics: a short product development cycle, flexibility, and a short sales cycle. The industrials must build a digital culture based on concepts like lean, agile, simplicity, responsiveness, and speed. That's a tall order for an established enterprise.

3. The incumbent's dilemma

Digital has the potential to disrupt industrial businesses. There are three ways digital strategy can cannibalize core industrial business. First, data and insights can help improve the productivity of machines; digital, therefore, has the potential to cannibalize future hardware sales. Second, data and insights increase the reliability of machines; digital therefore has the potential to cannibalize future service revenues. Third, software subscriptions and licenses might enable customers to do self-service. Current customers could terminate or renegotiate service contracts, and potential customers might not enter into service contracts at all. In short, it is very difficult for a company to disrupt itself.

The future of the industrial internet will involve partnerships across a variety of players including tech companies and industrial companies. The key issue: Who will assume the leadership position to extract maximum economic value in such an ecosystem? Will industrial companies take the lead? Or will the digital natives take the lead? Both have a chance.

If I were a betting man, I would place my bets on tech giants over industry incumbents. One factor that will favor digital companies in the industrial internet is the technological and scientific breakthroughs that level the playing field for newcomers. For example, breakthroughs in battery technology made electric cars possible. Electric cars are much simpler to design than cars with internal combustion engines, allowing Tesla and BYD to enter the market despite Ford's decades of expertise. Since electrification and driverless cars go together, other tech companies such as Google, Baidu, Apple, and Lyft will also be able to enter the automotive market. Similar technological changes in jet engines and agricultural tractors can allow tech giants to gain a foothold in these industries as well.

More importantly, Amazon or Google has the resources to acquire the capabilities to master the physics and acquire customer relationships and compete with the industrial giants in the industrial internet. They have enough resources to buy them, if needed.

Among the tech giants, Amazon is a likely winner in the industrial internet. It has successfully fused physical with digital. Amazon understands the economic laws of analog products and is not afraid of massive up-front investments and slower growth. Its acquisition of Whole Foods and experiments with Amazon Go grocery stores are an example. Amazon is the one company everyone's scared of, even industrial giants.

TAKEAWAYS

Tech giants have already disrupted industries from media to travel. But it's still too early to declare a winner in the race for the industrial internet: products that have physical components, "smart" components, and connectivity.

- ✓ If digital natives want to lead in the industrial internet, they need to overcome three barriers: the physics of the hardware, earning customer trust, and difficulty in sharing risks with partners they know little about.

- ✓ Industrial giants need to overcome three different barriers: attracting software talent, learning and operating a digital culture, and unwillingness to risk cannibalizing their core businesses.

- ✓ Amazon is a likely winner in the industrial internet, as it has already successfully fused physical with digital. Amazon understands the economic laws of analog products and is not afraid of massive up-front investments and slower growth.

Adapted from "Can Anyone Stop Amazon from Winning the Industrial Internet?" on hbr.org, February 2, 2018 (product #H0459N).

11

WHAT TO LEARN FROM THE GROCERY STORES HOLDING THEIR OWN AGAINST AMAZON

by Amit Sharma

The fight for the U.S. grocery industry has just begun. Amazon has shaken up the playing field, but traditional grocers have been slow to embrace technologies for online ordering, fulfillment, and delivery. Today online orders make up just 2% of grocery sales (in retail overall, the number is 10%). But e-commerce is quickly growing: Some analysts estimate that by 2025, 20% of grocery purchases will be made online.

And although Amazon/Whole Foods looms large, the e-commerce giant is far from the decided winner. In 2018, Walmart, Kroger, Costco, and Target drove down costs and introduced delivery capabilities in new regions, cutting into Amazon's market share. Meanwhile, new business models thrived. Instacart, for example, secured a $7.6 billion valuation and a loyal following by building a platform for grocery delivery and partnering with more than 300 retailers.

Instacart's success underscores what may be the most important point about the grocery industry's current state: Most shoppers today are not loyal to a single store or chain. The nature of customer loyalty is changing as shoppers get more comfortable buying groceries online— prioritizing convenience, choice, and ease over physical proximity to a store. As consumers become more sophisticated, retailers need to inspire lasting loyalty across their customer base. To do it, they should offer flexibility, proactively communicate about order status and other details, and build emotional connections with shoppers.

Flexibility is a big factor in repeat purchases, because consumers want to shop on their terms. In a study by my company, Narvar, 80% of shoppers said they're more likely to buy repeatedly from retailers that offer a range of convenient, flexible delivery options. Only 3% said such options have no impact on their likelihood to buy again. Shoppers want to choose when and how they get their groceries, whether it's same-day delivery; in-store, curbside, or drive-through pickup; or delivery to a convenient location, like a school or an office building. Grocers should aim to be able to bring products to their customers no matter where they are.

Walmart offers the leading example of this strategy. The company uses its dense network of stores as fulfillment centers and trains thousands of personal shoppers to pick high-quality meat and produce. On Walmart .com or through the Walmart Grocery app, shoppers can reserve a time for free pickup at their local store and have their groceries brought to their car. Walmart invested significantly in last-mile grocery delivery, partnering with companies including Postmates, DoorDash, and Uber to expand its same-day delivery service from 6 metro areas to more than 100.

These investments seem to be paying off. The company grabbed market share from Amazon and outperformed analyst expectations. In a 2018 survey, more consumers said they shop exclusively at Walmart than at any other retailer except Amazon.[1] And during the last quarter of 2018, Walmart's digital sales rose 43%, which the company attributed to two things: strong growth in grocery delivery and pickup services and a broader product selection on its website.

Communication is another important, and often overlooked, part of keeping customers happy. As people have grown accustomed to constant text conversations and Slack messages, they've come to expect brands to always be available, too. They want timely, accurate, and helpful information; some may prefer emails with recipes and promotions, while others may want pertinent updates through text messages or push notifications. Grocers should ask customers for permission to message them through different formats and give them control over how often and in what ways they receive information.

Proactive communication pays dividends in loyalty: Our study found that 81% of people are more likely to purchase again from a retailer that keeps them updated on the progress of an order. Shoppers want to be kept in the loop, so it's particularly important that companies reach out if something goes wrong.

Grocers can learn from innovators that are building direct lines of communication with their customers. They might take inspiration from the direct-to-consumer e-commerce startup Iris Nova, whose Dirty Lemon brand sells wellness drinks with ingredients like charcoal and turmeric. Iris Nova is on track to reach $100 million in revenue by 2021, driven by its text-based ordering system. Once customers register their account with a phone number, they can order by simply sending a text message. Since the company was founded in 2015, 90% of its orders have been processed through text. Once a customer orders, Dirty Lemon texts back to confirm the shipment and then sends delivery updates the same way, using the occasional emoji to create a casual rapport that works for its brand and younger-skewing audience.

Another example is Honey Baked Ham, which ships 700,000 hams every year, primarily around the holidays. (Disclosure: Honey Baked Ham is a client of Narvar.) The company takes steps to assure customers they're in good hands every step of the way. After customers click "buy," they receive a branded shipping confirmation from Honey Baked Ham, rather than a generic email from a carrier. Customers can click through to a tracking page that includes product recommendations and tips for storing and serving their ham. In 2017, Honey Baked Ham boosted its revenue by $2 million over three months by communicating directly with customers and reducing "Where is my order?" inquiries.

Emotional connection is another driver of loyalty; our survey found that 50% of consumers are more likely to buy again from a brand that connects with them emotionally or reflects their values. While good communication and flexibility are foundational to loyalty, grocers should also consider how they're making customers feel. A 2018 consumer survey by C Space found that shoppers were more likely to recommend and purchase repeatedly from brands that made them feel respected and understood.[2] The study also found that these measures of positive emotion were correlated with a company's growth.

And people *are* emotionally connected to grocers, as utilitarian as grocery shopping may seem. For example, Trader Joe's, which ranked highly in the C Space study, inspires loyalty by creating an enjoyable shopping atmosphere. A 2018 Forrester survey of 287 brands rated Trader Joe's first in positive customer experiences, and the company regularly outranks other grocery chains in sales per square foot. Trader Joe's fans closely follow new product releases, request stores in their towns, and have even created their own community on Reddit.

Trader Joe's doesn't offer grocery delivery, but it has created such a personal and enjoyable shopping experience that customers actually want to visit its stores. Everything at Trader Joe's is designed to make grocery shopping feel more friendly, personal, and laid-back, including its flexible return policies, free samples, quirky product labels, fast checkout, and helpful employees. The associates, called "crew members," are happy—Trader Joe's has made Glassdoor's list of Top 100 Best Places to Work five times since 2010—and create a feeling of community by talking with shoppers and recommending their favorite products. "Friendliness and service" earned Trader Joe's the top ranking in a 2018 study of shoppers' favorite grocery brands.[3]

Grocers need to offer their customers more than points-based customer loyalty programs, which are no longer a competitive differentiator. Most grocery chains offer similar benefits and do little to foster an emotional connection between a shopper and a brand. A study by Accenture found that 78% of shoppers abandon loyalty programs after signing up.

By investing in the factors that build long-lasting loyalty instead of transactional programs that most people ignore, grocers can attract repeat buyers and brand advocates. As shoppers expect more from the brands they do business with, they will prioritize their experience with a company, both online and in person, over everything else. The companies that offer people the most flexibility, communicate directly and effectively, and connect with them emotionally will emerge as the winners.

TAKEAWAYS

Even though Amazon acquired Whole Foods Market, there is plenty of room for smaller grocers to thrive in the fight for the U.S. grocery industry. Other industries can learn from these stores as they reinvent themselves to maintain their positions amid the tech giants.

- ✓ Grocery shoppers want options, especially around how and where they receive deliveries. They value personalized, proactive communication from stores and want grocers to make them feel good, whether that comes from friendly employees, welcoming store layouts, or generous return policies. Grocers that invest in these have the greatest chance of fending off new entrants.

- ✓ Across industries, customers increasingly expect more from the brands they do business with, and their loyalty is influenced by their experiences, both online and in person. By moving away from transactional relationships and toward building connections with customers, companies can attract repeat buyers and brand advocates.

✓ Companies that offer the most flexibility, communicate directly and effectively, and connect with
   them emotionally will emerge as the winners.

NOTES

1. Adam Blair, "Study: Amazon and Walmart Top Retail
Loyalty List," *Retail TouchPoints*, July 2, 2018, https://www
.retailtouchpoints.com/features/trend-watch/study-amazon-and
-walmart-top-retail-loyalty-list.

2. "Customer, Experienced," C Space, October 2018, https://
learn.cspace.com/hubfs/C_Space_Reports/CUSTOMER
_EXPERIENCED_2018.pdf.

3. Philip Cop, "Trader Joe's Success Formula and What Can Other
Retailers Learn from It," *TotalRetail*, September 6, 2018, https://www
.mytotalretail.com/article/trader-joes-success-formula-and-what
-can-other-retailers-can-learn-from-it/.

*Adapted from "What the Grocery Stores Holding Their Own Against Amazon Are
Doing Right," on hbr.org, April 12, 2019 (product #H04WGO).*

About the Contributors

JULIAN BIRKINSHAW is Deputy Dean and Professor of Strategy and Entrepreneurship at the London Business School. He is the author of *Fast/Forward: Make Your Company Fit for the Future.*

LARRY DOWNES is a coauthor of *Pivot to the Future: Discovering Value and Creating Growth in a Disrupted World.* His earlier books include *Big Bang Disruption, The Laws of Disruption,* and *Unleashing the Killer App* (Harvard Business School Press, 2000).

WALTER FRICK is an editor at Quartz and was formerly the deputy editor of hbr.org.

WILLIAM A. GALSTON is a senior fellow at the Brookings Institution. He spent nearly three decades teaching and conducting political science research at the University of Texas and the University of Maryland. He has participated in six presidential campaigns and spent two and a half years in the Clinton White House.

DIPAYAN GHOSH is a Shorenstein Fellow and codirector of the Platform Accountability Project at the Harvard Kennedy School. He was a technology and economic policy adviser in the Obama White House, and formerly served as an adviser on privacy and public policy issues at Facebook. He is the author of *Terms of Disservice*. Follow him on Twitter @ghoshd7.

VIJAY GOVINDARAJAN is the Coxe Distinguished Professor of Management at Dartmouth's Tuck School of Business. He is the author of *The Three-Box Solution* and *The Three-Box Solution Playbook* (Harvard Business Review Press, 2016, 2020).

CLARA HENDRICKSON is a research assistant at the Brookings Institution.

MARCO IANSITI is the David Sarnoff Professor of Business Administration at Harvard Business School, where he heads the Technology and Operations Management Unit and the Digital Initiative. He has advised many companies in the technology sector, including Microsoft, Facebook, and Amazon. He is a coauthor, with Karim R. Lakhani, of *Competing in the Age of AI* (Harvard Business Review Press, 2020).

MICHAEL G. JACOBIDES holds the Sir Donald Gordon Chair for Entrepreneurship and Innovation at the London Business School.

KARIM R. LAKHANI is the Charles Edward Wilson Professor of Business Administration and the Dorothy and Michael Hintze Fellow at Harvard Business School. He is also the founding director of the Harvard Innovation Science Laboratory. He is a coauthor, with Marco Iansiti, of *Competing in the Age of AI* (Harvard Business Review Press, 2020).

DARRELL K. RIGBY is a partner in the Boston office of Bain & Company. He heads the firm's global innovation practice. He is a coauthor of *Doing Agile Right: Transformation Without Chaos* (Harvard Business Review Press, 2020).

AMIT SHARMA is the founder and CEO of Narvar, a post-purchase experience platform, and a former executive at Apple and Walmart.

MAURICE E. STUCKE is a cofounder of the Konkurrenz Group and a law professor at the University of Tennessee.

DAVID WESSEL is a senior fellow in economic studies at the Brookings Institution and director of the Hutchins

Center on Fiscal and Monetary Policy, which he joined after 30 years on the staff of the *Wall Street Journal*. He is the author of two *New York Times* best-sellers: *In Fed We Trust: Ben Bernanke's War on the Great Panic* (2009) and *Red Ink: Inside the High Stakes Politics of the Federal Budget* (2012) and has shared two Pulitzer Prizes.

DENISE LEE YOHN is a leading authority on positioning great brands and building exceptional organizations and has 25 years of experience working with world-class brands including Sony and Frito-Lay. Denise is a consultant, speaker, and author of *What Great Brands Do: The Seven Brand-Building Principles That Separate the Best from the Rest* and *FUSION: How Integrating Brand and Culture Powers the World's Greatest Companies.*

HOWARD YU is the author of *LEAP: How to Thrive in a World Where Everything Can Be Copied*, and LEGO professor of management and innovation at the IMD business school in Switzerland. In 2015, Yu was featured in Poets & Quants as one of the Best 40 Under 40 Professors. He was shortlisted for the 2017 Thinkers50 Innovation Award, and in 2018 appeared on the Thinkers50 Radar list of 30 management thinkers "most likely to shape the future of how organizations are managed and led."

Index

Is Your Business Ready for the Future?

If you enjoyed this book and want more on today's pressing business topics, turn to other books in the **Insights You Need** series from *Harvard Business Review*. Featuring HBR's latest thinking on topics critical to your company's success—from Blockchain and Cybersecurity to AI and Agile—each book will help you explore these trends and how they will impact you and your business in the future.

Engage with HBR content the way you want, on any device.

With HBR's new subscription plans, you can access world-renowned **case studies** from Harvard Business School and receive **four free eBooks**. Download and customize prebuilt **slide decks and graphics** from our **Visual Library**. With HBR's archive, top 50 best-selling articles, and five new articles every day, HBR is more than just a magazine.

Subscribe Today
hbr.org/success